The Fun Side of the Wall

Baby Boomer Retirement in Mexico

Travis Scott Luther

THE FUN SIDE OF THE WALL
Baby Boomer Migration into Mexico

ISBN: 978-1-64764-001-9 - Hardcover
         978-1-64764-002-6 - Paperback
         978-1-64764-003-3 - Ebook

NHSO

The Fun Side of the Wall

For Henry and Benjamin.

May learning be your first true love.

CHAPTERS

Introduction

Who Should Read This Book

People Considering Retirement in Mexico

Retirees Living in Mexico

Researchers Investigating Baby Boomers, Retirement, and Non-Traditional Retirement Models

PART I. THE STATE OF RETIREMENT

CHAPTER 1

An Author's Journey – Stranger in a Strange Land

CHAPTER 2

Defining U.S. Baby Boomers

The Leading Edge

The Trailing Edge

Demography

Family Structure

Women

CHAPTER 3

A History of Retirement in the United States

Historical Perspective

Places and Communities

Traditional Financing

CHAPTER 4

A Financial Profile of U.S. Baby Boomers

> Savings
>
> Retirement
>
> Home Ownership
>
> Debt & Assets

PART II. WHO WOULD WANT TO LEAVE THE U.S.?

CHAPTER 5

Increased Interest in Retiring Abroad

> Cable Shows, Websites, Books and More…
>
> Growth in Out-Migration Over the Last 20 Years
>
> A History of Migration into Mexico

CHAPTER 6

The Mexico Boomers - Research Findings

> Methodology
>
> Profile & Demographic Findings
>
> Hypothesizing Motivations to Leave the United States

PART III. THE MEXICO BOOMERS – WHY THEY LEAVE

CHAPTER 7

Why They Leave

> Hypothesis 1: Money
>
> Cost of Living, Meaningful Employment
>
> & Early Retirement

INTRODUCTION

Who Should Read This Book
    People Considering Retirement in Mexico
    Retirees Living in Mexico
    Researchers Investigating Baby Boomers, Retirement,
    and Non-Traditional Retirement Models

This book is the culmination of 8 years of travel and research related to U.S. Baby Boomer expatriates who made the decision to leave the United States and retire in Mexico. The foundation of this book originally appeared in my Master's thesis, published through the Sociology Department of the University of Colorado Denver.

In my thesis, I set out to discover what motivated tens of thousands of U.S. Baby Boomers to leave their homes, their country, and their families to retire in Mexico. My hypothesis was pretty simple: I suspected that Baby Boomers who were financially affected by the brutal 2008 recession were leaving the United States in an attempt to stretch retirement dollars further in Mexico. On that suspicion, I was right. (Not only was I right, but I under-predicted how far those U.S. dollars were going.) However, my research revealed two big surprises – first, the extent to which ageism in the United States motivates people to leave, and second, that U.S. Baby Boomers are not just moving to Mexico independently, but that they are moving into vibrant expatriate communities, with thousands of members, that have existed for over half a century.

With regard to their finances, U.S. Baby Boomers are indeed getting more for their money in Mexico. Consumer prices alone average nearly 65% more in the U.S. than in Mexico. Healthcare costs in Mexico range from one-fifth to one-third of those in the United States. People in the U.S. pay 200% more for rent on comparable housing, and they are not even getting the luxuries that come with many Mexican rentals, including staff to assist with the house. Throughout this book, we will explore the ways Baby Boomers are saving money, how they are navigating the healthcare system, and the role finances play in their quality of life.

Ageism proved to be a topic of significant frustration among the Baby Boomers I surveyed. I concluded that, over the last decade, social media has made us increasingly aware of marginalized groups. Caitlyn Jenner tweeted a conversation about gender identity into nearly every home. The grassroots response to recent police shootings of African Americans has been hash-tagged and organized online. We show approval of the U.S. Supreme Court's decision to allow gay marriage by updating our Facebook profile pictures with rainbows. And we are quick to expose people and companies guilty of "body shaming" by calling them out online to answer for their insensitivities. Through social media, a new generation is engaging in societal issues – both old and new. However, the subjects of this book insist that there are few coming to the defense of the aging population or negating the stereotypes held against them. Perhaps that is because no matter which specific social cause we individually hold dear, collectively we continue to be a culture obsessed with youth.

While this obsession may seem to some an obvious and harmless ploy to sell more skin-care products, researchers suggest it has a real emotional and financial effect on our older population. Ageism, and the stereotypes associated with getting older, makes our aging population feel as if they live in a world where they have no value. They express frustration that in their older years they are not invited to participate in the society that they helped make great. They do not see the media portray beauty in people who look like they do. They are phased out or are asked to take early retirement from companies that they helped build. They are passed over for promotions, and frequently, they are unable to secure meaningful employment because of stereotypes related to their age. For some in this book there is a feeling that the United States is at war with old age. Rather than become a casualty of this war, they have decided to leave the U.S. in search of more neutral surroundings.

When I began looking for expatriates in Mexico, I thought I would find tiny isolated pockets of Baby Boomers – watching TV, pinching their pennies, and taking it easy. In fact, one of my graduate advisor's concerns was that I would not find enough "Mexico Boomers" to create a significant sample. To our surprise, what I uncovered were many large communities and tens of thousands of U.S. retirees. In the Lake Chapala region, there are estimated to be 6,000 full-time expatriate residents, swelling to over 20,000 in the winter. To the east, San Miguel de Allende is home to about 5,000 expatriates and growing. From the northern tip of Baja all the way to the Yucatan peninsula in the south, there are over one million U.S. citizens living in Mexico right now.

These communities of expatriates are not living strictly amongst themselves. Over decades, they have integrated themselves into existing Mexican communities – not living on the periphery but co-existing with locals, forming friendships, sharing in each other's art and culture, running businesses together, building charitable organizations together, and even getting married. These communities were quite the opposite of the elitist isolation I admittedly expected to find. I also found that for most of these Mexico Boomers, Mexico was not just a place to live on the cheap but a country they now considered home. The vast majority of the Americans I surveyed said

3

that even if money was not an issue, they would not give up their Mexican communities and return to the United States.

Let me be clear: Retirement in Mexico is not for everyone. Permanent migration into Mexico is a very personal decision. The motivations for such a move vary tremendously from person to person. Much like some people prefer living on farms over big cities, or vacations on snow-covered mountains over Caribbean cruises, choosing a place to live and retire depends on what you want, what you need, and what you are comfortable with – and, perhaps more importantly, what you are not.

There are some shared experiences that come with living in the United States that are just flat out different in Mexico. Probably the most striking is the slower pace of life. A leisurely life may sound great when you decide to bury your watch in the sand and just lay on the beach until you feel like going home, but it might not be so great when you are waiting for someone to come repair your broken shower. It was not unusual for people I interviewed to comment that things just take longer in Mexico. Lines are longer, the mail takes longer, repairs take longer, etc. That pace takes some getting used to – and, if you are not a patient person (or do not have the patience to become one) then Mexico might not be for you. However, I found that this very pace that was so frustrating to some was also a magnet for others. "We don't sweat the small stuff here," I heard in various forms over and over. "If it's not a big deal, it's not a big deal." There are other experiences that remind U.S. retirees living in Mexico that they are "not in Kansas anymore." I will be sure to discuss those later in the book so that if you are considering retirement in Mexico, you can do so with eyes wide open.

Finally, I want to be up front about one more thing. There are quite a few books out there about retiring in Mexico, traveling in Mexico, and sightseeing in Mexico. These are mostly "how-to" guides built on authors' personal experiences or popular wisdom. My book is not an attempt to give you instructions on "how-to" do anything. My book is different from other books available on the subject in that it is research based. That does not mean it is boring. This book is full of engaging stories, personal experiences, and travel narratives. But while some books might take a few experiences and generalize them to an entire population, I'm digging a little deeper. Rather than taking what people say at face value, in this book I study what they actually do – and how circumstances at home and abroad affect those decisions. I am also examining that action within a large group of expatriates, not just through a few friendly interviews. So, while you will certainly learn a lot about Mexican geography and some popular destinations, we will be learning more about what Mexico has to offer people on a more permanent basis, especially for those in search of meaningful community and a higher quality of life.

For me, the great joy of books is their ability to take us to other places and other worlds. Whether fiction or nonfiction, books will always remain that great window through which we safely peer into the lives of strangers. I hope this book will be one of those windows for you. It was an eye-opening opportunity for me, and I am grateful I stumbled upon the subject. I consider it a great honor to be able to introduce you to the "Mexico Boomers" and the diverse communities they are creating and living in.

PART I.

THE STATE OF RETIREMENT

In their own words...

When Fabian was in high school, she met a 20-something international soccer star who had been recruited to play in the United States. "This was the time of Pele and other big stars really starting to create an interest in soccer in the United States. He had been asked to play in the U.S. in hopes of making the sport more popular. His team was based in our little Massachusetts town," she recalled with a laugh. "My high school girlfriends and I had no lack of interest in them and they had no lack of interest in us." When her new boyfriend decided to return to Europe, he asked her to go with him. She was 19 years old. They married and when she was 21, they had a son while living in Scotland. They moved around Europe a bit. "But," she says, "professional athletes get a lot of attention. He had plenty from other women, and eventually we had to part."

For a while she went it alone in Europe, living in Denmark and Greece. She worked as a tour guide in Spain and Portugal before returning to the east coast of the United States. Eventually her wanderlust pulled her to California's Napa Valley where she would spend the next 12 years.

In October of 1999, Fabian was working as an event coordinator. She arranged business retreats for Silicon Valley executives who were still unaware that their tech bubble was about to burst. "There was tons of money everywhere, and these guys were spending it like crazy on these lavish wine country business retreats." In addition to coordinating business meetings and special events, Fabian had the daytime responsibility of entertaining the executives' wives. "I would take them on winery tours and to fancy lunches. It was really quite the life."

While Fabian enjoyed her work, the company owner was a completely different story. "I had this boss who was a real asshole. He was so verbally abusive. I just couldn't understand how a man could speak to a 40-something year-old woman the way he spoke to me." One October morning, Fabian was sitting at her

7

computer, learning new design software. She was stumped. "My boss walked over to me, looked down at my computer and asked me why I was so stupid." She pauses. "That was really it for me. That was the day everything changed."

After work, Fabian drove to a local yoga studio. "I'd really just started going. This was only my second or third time ever trying it." Fabian laughs now. "It was really my boss who drove me to yoga because he made me so stressed out!"

She rolled out her mat, laid down in Child's pose, and before the class had even started, tears began to pour from her eyes. "It was rather incredible," she says. When class was over, she walked out to her car. "I looked up and realized I didn't feel any stress at all. I just felt so peaceful." She began to cry again. "This was the first time in my life I ever felt this calm. I had never believed that was possible, and now here I was knowing it was."
It was this experience that began her quest to live in a perpetual state of ease, for stress to become the exception, for solace to become the rule.

She quit her job and started a 12-month work-study program in Big Sur, developing a personal yoga practice and completing the credentialing required to eventually teach others. But when school ended, she couldn't find work. "It was so disappointing. I knew what I wanted to do, and there was just nowhere to do it."

She had a girlfriend, a painter, who had moved to San Miguel de Allende, Mexico, a few years earlier. Her friend was insistent that Fabian join her. But Fabian had no money. She had just spent the last year in school. So, on a whim, she asked a good friend, a chocolatier, if he might be able to help her out. "There was a knock at the door. A deliveryman handed me a box of chocolates. I opened it and it exploded with $100 bills. It was amazing." She immediately sold her car and everything else she had. "I wasn't scared," she says. "Sure, I tried to do some of my own research on Mexico, but by this point in my life I had also really come to trust my friends, my wanderlust, and yoga." She arrived in San Miguel de Allende in 2000 with about $2000 and one suitcase.

8

"Suddenly everything was easy," she says. "I wanted to teach yoga. There was one other woman teaching yoga in town. Rather than compete, we partnered up. I was working immediately. I was doing what I love. There were tons of empty houses that other expats desperately wanted someone to live in and take care of. I lived in beautiful homes for free."

Today, Fabian has her own yoga studio nestled inside a bed and breakfast, with a pool outside her front door. A fragrant smell of flowers and the polite chirp of birds drifts through her glass doors. "Yes," she says. "It's less expensive to live here. I have a $300.00 apartment with a view more gorgeous than anything I could have ever afforded in Europe. I work from 9:00 a.m. to 11:30 a.m. I have enough money to live and even to travel back home two or three times a year to visit my sisters. But what I really have is freedom. I have my own time to pursue my own interests. I can write. I can walk. Most of my day is spent doing whatever it is I feel like doing. That's why I'm here. That's why I stay. I'm never leaving Mexico."

There's another reason she stays. "I can't put my finger on it," she says. "It's just a feeling. There's something crumbling up there." She points north to the United States. "And it's shaking some of us out."

CHAPTER 1

Stranger in a Strange Land
       An Author's Journey
       Methodology
       Research Goals

I was not born a person predisposed to exotic adventures. I grew up in a rural area of the United States, within an agricultural region known as the Palouse. This area rests on the central border of Washington and Idaho. I lived in towns named Steptoe, St. John, Albion, Colfax, and Pullman. Unless you are from the area, you probably have not heard of them. The communities I grew up in were generally small, insulated, conservative, and working class.

The 1980s and early 1990s made up my formative years. This period encompassed the end of the Cold War, seemingly endless civil wars in Africa, the Bosnian Genocide, the narco wars of Central America, and the first Persian Gulf War. It was during this time, as an adolescent that I came to generalize the world outside of the United States as dangerous and stupid, having little to offer a person like me.

I carried this view, largely unchallenged, into my early adult years. In 1998 and 1999, I attended Washington State University in Pullman, Washington. After a year, I dropped out – missing an opportunity to add to my knowledge of the world. In 2004, I had a chance to move to Denver, Colorado, with a good friend and return to school. Once in Denver, finishing college became my top priority.

Returning to school as an adult motivated me to access information and ideas that I had previously locked out. For the first time in my life, I became far more inquisitive than certain.

While completing my general education requirements, I stumbled upon and formed an intense romance with sociological theory. In fact, the theories and subject matter in sociology were so interesting to me, that I changed my major from Marketing to Behavioral Science.

During this time, I also stumbled upon and formed an intense romance with an attorney. I had a slight knack for technology and art, and, as I finished my bachelor's degree, I started building a nice little business for myself, serving the technology and graphic design needs of the legal community. It was not long before my services were in high demand. Soon I was beginning to feel overwhelmed with both school and business, so I started to contract some of my work out to other technology professionals in Denver.

In the spring of 2006, I was sitting in the Denver International Airport, waiting to get on a plane for a visit back to Washington. Bored to death, I wandered into a terminal bookstore. With no real knowledge of the book's contents, I bought The World is Flat by Thomas L. Friedman.[1] I became completely engrossed and read like I had never read before. The World is Flat vividly revealed to me a world outside the United States more modern than I had ever considered. Friedman described the hustle and bustle of international entrepreneurs in a way with which I could personally identify. Friedman interviewed young people growing businesses abroad who were struggling with some of the same challenges I was struggling with as a young entrepreneur in the United States. Through his book, Friedman had connected me to the international

---

[1] Friedman, T.L. (2005). *The World Is Flat*. Farrar, Straus and Giroux. New York.

entrepreneurial community in a very personal way. Additionally, the book turned upside down every preconceived notion I had about American Exceptionalism. For the first time in my life, Friedman had me questioning whether or not the United States truly offered the best of everything.

The effect of The World is Flat simmered inside me for a year. Then in 2007, Timothy Ferriss released a business/lifestyle book titled The 4-Hour Work Week.[2] The premise of Ferriss' book is that many of the tasks in our businesses and our personal lives can be outsourced to others. According to Ferris, doing so frees up your time, improves your quality of life, and allows you to do more of what you want to do – not what you have to do. Ferriss' and Friedman's books are important influences on this book because they both discuss the convergence of technology and outsourcing, specifically the increasing availability of fast and low-cost internet connections (it is also this convergence, I will argue later, that has accelerated retirement abroad). What Ferriss provided in his book, that Friedman did not, was actual contact information and web-based portals for international outsourcing and international living. Like Walt Whitman said of Ralph Waldo Emerson, "I was simmering, simmering, simmering, Emerson brought me to a boil."[3] Friedman had me simmering, but it was Ferriss who brought me to a boil. Armed with Ferriss's resources, I aggressively began to seek out opportunities to connect with entrepreneurs outside of the United States.

In 2008, I started outsourcing some of my business projects to India, Eastern Europe, and South America. I also used these outsourcing experiments as an opportunity to try and connect on a

---

[2] Ferriss, T. (2007). *The 4-Hour Work Week*. Crown Publishers: New York.

[3] Trowbridge, John Townsend (1902, February). Reminiscences of Walt Whitman. *The Atlantic Monthly*.

personal level with the foreigners I was working with, asking all sorts of questions about what life was like where they lived. Not all of my outsourcing experiments were successful or financially advantageous, but they completely changed the way I viewed the world outside the United States. I started focusing a lot more of my time reading about international history. Because of its close proximity to the United States, I started using Mexico and South America as the focal point of most of my remaining undergraduate research projects.

By 2009, I was convinced that I had been both completely ignorant for the last 20 years and that the world was rapidly changing in my favor. Here I was, a 28-year-old technology entrepreneur who had found a way to turn the entire world into a collaborative resource. By this time, I had also entered the Master's of Sociology program at the University of Colorado Denver. My wife and I had our first son and another one on the way. Recognizing that I had grown-up a bit sheltered, I began to consider how a strictly U.S.-based life would affect my children and their perceptions of the world. Finding opportunities to expose my children to other cultures lead me to seek the whereabouts of expatriate enclaves. I started to explore the possibility of some long-term international sabbaticals for our family. It was during this period that my personal interest in locating expatriate groups coincided with having to make a final determination about the direction of my Master's thesis. As a result of this personal and scholastic collision, the most basic premise of this book was born: Why would anyone want to move away from the United States?

In graduate school, you do not actually get to ask and answer questions as broad as, "Why would anyone want to move away from the United States?" In fact, most of one's time in graduate school is spent panicking about how to come up with a simple enough question to get you out of graduate school on time. My original question fell into the category of those too broad to get you out of graduate school on time, and, thus, had to be pared down to a few reasonable goals and one very specific demographic: Baby Boomers. I chose Baby Boomers because they were all the rage at the time. From being subject to former President Obama's "Death Panels" to wiping out Social Security, Baby Boomers were promised to have an unprecedented impact on the next 30 years, and I wanted to keep a close eye on them.

First, I decided to conduct a pilot study that would isolate one community in Mexico where U.S. citizens were permanently migrating. Second, I would try and confirm the prevailing popular wisdom that money made them leave. This second part created quite a conundrum. A lot of people, inside and outside of the U.S., have come to the somewhat warranted conclusion that the only thing Americans care about is money. So, the conclusion that money could also have the power to drive them out of their home country was quite controversial. If my hypothesis was correct, then one would have to conclude that, for Mexico Boomers at least, the love of money had surpassed everything else that bound someone to this country and made them "American" – even baseball! If my hypothesis was wrong, and money was not the primary reason Baby Boomers were leaving the United States, then something (or some things) that once made our country "exceptional" must be in decay and no longer worth staying around for. But what?

An Author's Journey

To get answers, I located an isolated group of Baby Boomer retirees, bought plane tickets for my wife and I, and flew to Mexico to ask them why they left the United States. This first trip to Mexico was way back in 2009. Except a 15-hour trip I took to Canada in 1999, this was the very first time I had ventured outside of the United States. And for all of my research and interaction with the people I was about to meet, for all my newly acquired open-mindedness, I will

14

admit that I still arrived in Mexico with more than a few closely held stereotypes. For example, while at the Mexican airport I viewed anything remotely in disrepair as evidence of lower safety standards while completely ignoring the dilapidation of LAX. I catalogued the fact that I had to make a big, up-front insurance deposit on my rental car as the swindle of two helpless Americans rather than local law. I saw the roadside water, juice, and fruit vendors as a sign of high unemployment rather than just people working their actual jobs. I still hadn't completely broken myself of the notion that if things were different in Mexico then they must be worse than the United States. But different isn't always worse. In fact, sometimes it's better.

I tell you this because I realize I shared an attitude with most people who make quick trips to Mexico. Most Americans who visit our southern neighbor do so on vacation. In fact, nearly 29 million Americans visited Mexico in 2015 (I was one of them).[4] While we are there, we want to be served and have the times of our lives. We want a reality that is far better than the one we left back home. Because of this, our orientation toward Mexico and the people who live there is not one of neighbors and community but rather one of servitude. Through travel brochures and cruise deals, Mexico exists in the American mind to make us happy. Anything that falls short of that promise becomes a reason to frown on the whole country. But that's tantamount to being a foreign tourist frustrated with the people of Seattle because they don't have a Disneyland. The entire United States is not Disneyland! Good vacation marketing might be one reason for some of my own hesitation to see Mexico for what it truly was. The media certainly explains another.

---

[4] Martín, H. (2015, July 30). U.S. residents flocked to Mexico in record numbers last year. *Los Angeles Times*.

When I left for Mexico, there were two prevailing themes about the country being looped in U.S. media. First, that it was home to a raging drug war where hundreds of people were killed in the streets daily. Second, all Mexicans wanted to leave Mexico and sneak into the United States. So, when I left the Guadalajara airport for our downtown hotel, I expected to find throngs of poor people beating on my car asking for money or a lift to the U.S. border. I also thought I would see teams of heavily armed police racing through the streets in the back of flatbed pick-up trucks. I found neither.

What I did find my first morning in Mexico was clean-cut uniformed school kids waiting at a bus stop, men and women in business suits sucking down coffee as they paced up and down the city sidewalks, and older people reading newspapers in the park. It was all so…normal! My wife and I ventured to a sidewalk café for breakfast where I expected to stick out like a sore thumb. I felt very self-conscious about my "Americanism," and thought I might get some sympathetic treatment for it. Our server came to our table and, in perfect Spanish, asked me something I didn't understand. I delivered back that classic line (in English) that Americans around the world are so loved for, "Don't you speak English?" "No." was her answer. Now surely, she would be off to fetch the house translator so that he could walk me through the menu and make sure my order was prepared just the way I wanted, right? No. Our waitress just stood there, pen and notepad in hand, waiting for me to tell her what I wanted…in Spanish. I'm not exactly sure what I ordered, but I'm certain it was delicious. More importantly, this interaction seemed to give me permission to put my preconceived notions aside and seek out an authentic Mexico (and to my wife's great amusement, a commitment to cobble together some Spanish every chance I had).

After a couple of days exploring Guadalajara, we got in our car and headed south about 30 miles to the Lake Chapala region of Mexico. If you've ever done any kind of internet search related to

U.S. expats living in Mexico then you've undoubtedly discovered Lake Chapala. I had made appointments to meet with some of these folks and get to the bottom of why they had left the United States for Mexico.

The Lake Chapala region of Mexico is located in the western-pacific part of the country, a little over 100 miles directly east of Puerto Vallarta in the state of Jalisco. The region hugs Lake Chapala itself, which is Mexico's largest body of freshwater and the home of the Lake Chapala Society (LCS), an area non-profit that assists people moving into the Lake Chapala region from other countries.

As part of my preliminary investigation, I located an article by Dr. David Truly who had conducted previous research with some of the LCS membership. I called Dr. Truly, and he agreed to meet my wife and I in Lake Chapala. I did not know this at the time, but just six months earlier, Dr. Truly had made the decision himself to permanently move his own family to Lake Chapala. Now, this revelation has every appearance of a psychologist falling in love with her patient or a kidnapping victim starting to sympathize with his captors, but Truly is not too different from a lot of the people I eventually spoke to. Affectionately known in the area as the "Barefoot Professor," he is a liberal Caucasian with a hankering for adventure who had stumbled upon an inexpensive community that mirrored his own values and provided a pace of life he couldn't find in the United States. So, his move sounds pretty reasonable. But what made the professor unique was that he was in his 40's (a comparatively young age) and the fact that he moved to the area with two grade-school aged children. It is not unheard of to find U.S.-born kids going to school in Mexico – but it is unusual compared to the older retirees who make up a majority of the Lake Chapala residents.

The Barefoot Professor was key to the success of my Master's thesis and to the additional research that eventually led to the development of this book. He was a trusted visitor of the LCS, and an association with him gave me easy access to the LCS membership. He introduced me to all sorts of people living and doing business in the area and made them feel comfortable with my presence. Additionally, Dr. Truly's openness to guiding me in my study was personally reassuring, as there was no doubt I was a stranger in a strange land.

The original goals for my Master's thesis are not too different from the goals of this book: to provide an intimate look at the lives of Baby Boomers living in Mexico and to uncover their motivations for moving there. This book is different from my thesis in that it is an expanded look at Baby Boomers living all over Mexico – not just the LCS.

It is important to note that immediately after my first trip to Lake Chapala, my university initiated a research travel ban to Mexico. They did this out of safety concerns stemming from accelerated drug war violence (violence, I might add, that none of my study participants felt affected by or in danger of). This ban dramatically reduced the scope of my own research and made it impossible to uncover those organic developments that can spring from being embedded in a community you are studying. My data ended up coming from web surveys and internet interactions rather than from open-ended relationships I had hoped to establish through traveling the region.

I published my thesis in 2011 and graduated with my M.A. in Sociology that same year. While disappointed in the travel restrictions and the handcuffs it put on my project, I am very proud of my research, the motivations I uncovered, and my contribution to the limited study of out-migration that continues to exist today. But I always felt there was still more work to do.

Methodology

In 2017, I decided to dust off this manuscript and start thinking about ways it could be rewritten as an accessible book for people interested in the topic. There was something about the lack of deep personal narratives that made the idea of just rewriting what I already wrote feel very incomplete. So, I decided I would initiate a whole new study and some additional trips to Mexico. If I was ever going to be able to deliver something relevant, it had to be now. I hired one of my students to update some of the existing data and set off on my own gathering new information and finding new communities to interview.

In 2011, I dreaded being reliant on the internet. By 2017, it had become a treasure trove of organized expat communities and web directories for international living. In 2011, it took me weeks to conduct and collect the surveys that became the dataset for my original thesis. In 2017, I had already twice as many qualified respondents in just two days! Not only did I collect hundreds of responses, those responses came from over 30 different cities, towns, and regions of Mexico. As a result, the information in this book is the most extensive survey of Baby Boomer expats living in Mexico to date.

In addition to online surveys, I traveled to a number of well-known expat communities in Mexico to see how they changed since my original project. I wanted to assess any significant differences residents' attitudes compared to my initial trip. I also wanted the first-hand opportunity to hear the stories and reasons of those who had made the move, and poke around for anything I might have missed.

Finally, I conducted phone or online interviews with experts on the subject, both in the United States and Mexico. Those interviews helped me understand not only what the world is like for Baby Boomers in Mexico right now, but also what the world could look like for Baby Boomers just a few years down the road. As this generation becomes the largest single wave of retired people to ever live, they create a number of challenges. I don't think these are challenges we can't overcome, but they certainly can't be ignored.

Research Goals

The surveys I conducted in 2016 and 2017 mirror a lot of the questions I asked the Lake Chapala residents from 2009-2011. There are 65 questions, which cover a range of topics including simple demographics (age, race, gender, marital status, etc.), finances and income, community, public safety, ageism, materialism, and more.

As I previously mentioned, my research goals were to identify Baby Boomers who had permanently moved to Mexico and uncover what motivated them to do so. As part of that larger goal, I also wanted to answer some very specific questions about who these people are and to see if I could find any commonalities between them that could explain their decisions. To that end, I conducted a demographic survey, and where comparable data was available, this profile was compared to the demographic profile of retirees living in the United States. While not everyone was in alignment on all answers, there was certainly a prominent demographic profile that emerges. This profile, and all other findings of my research will be presented in Chapter 7.

Next, I wanted to understand the role that finances played in Baby Boomers' exit from the United States. To explore that motivation, I asked questions about participants' current financial status, how much money were they receiving every month, where that money came from, whether it was more or less than they expected to have when they were originally planning their retirements, and if money was of no consequence, would they still choose to live in Mexico?

I was also curious about what role strong communities played in their emigration. I asked what participants wanted out of a community, whether they thought they could find that in the United States, and how Mexico ranked on the community factors they reported to be most important.

During my first trip to Mexico, I heard a number of stories from people who claimed to have moved there after being forced into an early retirement. Issues of employment where never part of my original plan, but after hearing so much about it, I decided to include questions related to Baby Boomers' ability to find meaningful work.

Finally, I wanted to know how Baby Boomers in Mexico felt about stereotypes related to older people and seniors. Did they experience ageism or discrimination? Did they feel respected? Did they feel like they had a valuable role to play in society? Did they feel unfairly stigmatized? Did they want their retirement living dictated by city and community planners or did they want the freedom to create their own priorities? These are the questions that have been the most enlightening for me as a researcher because they have cut through a lot of conventional wisdom advanced by retirement planners in the United States. Also, as an unexpected outcome of this book, an important new question was raised: Is Mexico that much better than the United States or is the United States getting that much worse at confronting the issues important to retirees? That is a question you will have to answer for yourself, but I believe there is a lot of helpful information is this book to guide you.

Before we try and pinpoint exactly why Mexico Boomers have left the United States, let's first explore exactly who Baby Boomers are and how they differ from generations past and present.

In their own words...

As a child, Jan never went anywhere. Her parents were alcoholics, and her mother rarely left her bedroom. Jan was the oldest of five kids, so it was with a great deal of guilt that she moved herself into a church sponsored girls' home when she was 17 years old. She married young — first for five years, and then again for 31. She had two daughters. As an adult, she never ventured outside the United States. A Texas woman, she felt content with her family, her country, and her guns.

Jan went to nursing school. The last 15 years of her career she worked as a hospice nurse. Taking care of the dying is not for everyone, but it never bothered Jan. A woman of unabashed faith, she felt incredibly blessed to be one of the last intimate relationships her patients would have. But with that intimacy came confessions, and on top of the confessions, regrets. "I started to hear the same few things over and over again," Jan says. "People were begging me not to spend my life worrying about money, not to let others hold me down, and to go experience as much as I could for myself."

Jan started to take these comments more and more seriously. "When I was younger, it was easy to hear these things and brush them off," she says. "But as I got older, it hit home that someday it would be me lying in that bed. I wouldn't say I panicked, but I knew if I was going to do something incredible, I really had to start planning it right away."

She can't say where it started, but at some point, Jan knew that what she really wanted for her own life was to live in another country. "Once I made that decision, I subscribed to a bunch of international living magazines and spent all of my free time researching expats on the internet." She considered Panama, Costa Rica, and even Columbia. "But I just kept coming back to Mexico," she says. "It was close to Texas. It was easy to get online and meet other people living there, and there was just something reassuring about the community that was already established there."

"My family thought I was crazy," she says. "But I finally convinced my husband to take a trip there with me, just to check it out." As soon as they arrived, Jan felt like she was exactly where she needed to be. "My husband and I met with a builder and bought a home. I just knew this was what I wanted, and I wanted it as soon as possible." With the contract signed and construction beginning, Jan and her husband returned to Texas. "When we got back, I started to make all the arrangements to move. But something was off with my husband. He started to worry that we weren't ready, that we didn't have enough money, that we needed to work much longer than we really did." Jan says her husband kept putting off the move. "Finally, I asked him," she said. "If I back off and give you five more years to put everything in order, will you promise me you'll move to Mexico with me?" He couldn't promise. Jan was devastated. "I couldn't believe it. I really thought it was going to happen, and then he backed out. We cancelled the order on our house. Everything just stopped."

"And then I told myself, you have to do this. No regrets. You're moving to Mexico." And with that conviction, Jan calmly explained to her husband that this was something that she needed to do for herself. She needed to do it right then. She understood that this was not his dream. She also told him that though she wished she did not have to do it, they would be getting a divorce. "It was sad, but it was cordial. We weren't fighting. My husband understood that this was about me and not about him. We held hands as we stood in the courtroom and the judge finalized the paperwork. We went home and made love. I still love my ex-husband. It was never about that." A few months later, Jan was living in Mexico. "No regrets," she says, two years after the move. "I'm exactly where I need to be."

Today, Jan is a party planner who helps organize celebrations and get-togethers for other expats. She's learned Spanish, has no car, and takes taxis everywhere she goes. With some irony, and on her own, she was able to purchase the same condo she and her ex-husband had originally contracted to build a few years earlier. It *has a giant patio with an outdoor cooking area that Jan says she hopes to use to start a catering company someday.*

CHAPTER 2

Defining U.S. Baby Boomers
> The Leading & Trailing Edges
> Racial Diversity
> Family Structure
> Women

Who Are the U.S. Baby Boomers?

Baby Boomers, people born between 1946 and 1964, represent the largest birth cohort in our nation's history. Seventy-six million strong, the first half of this cohort has already entered retirement.[1] It is estimated that 10,000 Baby Boomers a day turn 65, a pattern that will continue through 2025.[2]

Sylvia F. Porter first noted the existence of a post-war birth boom in a column in the May 4, 1951, edition of the New York Post. She wrote her column in response to a 2.3-million population increase in the United States in the previous year. In 1966, Time magazine designated Baby Boomers (called "The Inheritors" at the time) as the magazine's "Man of the Year"[3] (somewhat ironically sandwiched between General Westmoreland in 1965 and President

---

[1] AARP. (1999). Baby Boomers Envision Their Retirement: An AARP Segmentation Analysis. Washington D.C. *Association for American Retired Persons*.

[2] Associated Press. (2010, December 27). 10,000 Boomers to Retire Each Day for 19 Years.

[3] Time Magazine. (1967, January 6). Twenty-five and under, man of the year.

Johnson in 1967[4] and the Vietnam War that would shape most of their lives).

The term "Baby Boomer," was not coined until the Washington Post used the phrase in news reports beginning in 1970. Once printed in the Post, "Baby Boomer" stuck around.

Baby Boomers are distinguished as a generational group based on a post-World War II birthrate that outpaced preceding and subsequent cohorts.[5] The distinction exists both in the marked increase in the birthrate itself as well as the extended length of time that the uptick endured (1946-1964). The United States was not alone in this phenomenon. In the United Kingdom, this post-war birth increase is called The Bulge. But perhaps nowhere else in the world was this growth as pronounced, or as recognized, as in the United States, where 65 million babies were born at a peak rate of seven[6] every second.

As a result of the Baby Boom, today there are more people retired (or facing retirement) than at any other time in history.[7] The U.S. population 65 or older has grown from 3 million in 1900 to over 35 million today.[8] Americans 65 or older reached 12.4% of the population in 2000 and are projected to grow an additional 20%, reaching 90 million by 2060.[9]

---

[4] Time Person of the Year. (2019, December 12). *In Wikipedia.*

[5] Colby, S.L. & Ortman, J.M. (2014, May). The Baby Boom cohort in the United States: 2012 to 2060: Population estimates and projections. *U.S. Department of Commerce Census Bureau.*

[6] Baby Boom. (2019, December 12). In *Wikipedia.*

[7] Moen, P., Huang, Q., Plassmann, V. & Dentinger, E. (2006). Deciding the Future: Do Dual-Earner Couples Plan Together for Retirement? *American Behavioral Scientist, 49*(10), 1422-1443.

[8] Wilmoth, J. E., Longino, C. F. Jr. (2006). Demographic Trends That Will Shape U.S. Policy in the Twenty-First Century. *Research on Aging, 28*(3), 269-288.

[9] Himes, C. (2001). Elderly Americans. *Population Bulletin, 56*(4), 3-40.

The Leading and Trailing Edge

Although the Baby Boom wave is generally considered to extend from 1946 until 1964, many who analyze the post-war birth cohort conclude that Baby Boomers might be better understood by distinguishing them into two sub-cohorts; the Leading Edge Baby Boomers (born between 1946 and 1955) and the Trailing Edge Baby Boomers (born between 1956 and 1964).[10]

Baby Boomers,[11] as a whole, share many of the same historical experiences. But it is important to note that the 18-year gap between the very first and the very last Baby Boomers often creates differing perspectives on politics, world events, and their own role in history.

When the first of the Leading Edge Boomers were turning 16 years old, they were doing Chubby Checker's Twist. By the time the last of the Trailing Edge had gone to prom, they were dancing to Blondie and Michael Jackson. In college, the Leading Edge was reading Jacqueline Susann's Valley of the Dolls while the Trailing Edge read Stephen King's Pet Sematary. For some Leading Edge, Lyndon Johnson was the first president they were old enough to vote for. For the Trailing Edge, it was Jimmy Carter or Ronald Reagan. Leading Edge Baby Boomers came of age during the Vietnam War, many were drafted and saw action in Southeast Asia. On the other hand, Trailing Edge Boomers were still just children, and none of them faced the threat of compulsory military service. Leading Edge Baby Boomers remember the assassination of President Kennedy. For the Trailing Edge Baby Boomers, Watergate was their coming-of-age event, laying the seeds of political cynicism that would come to pepper their politics.

---

[10] Howe, N. & Strauss, W. (1991). *Generations: The History of Americas Future, 1584 to 2069*. New York: William Morrow.

[11] Green, B. (2005, June 20). Leading-edge vs. trailing-edge Boomers. *Boomers: A trip into the heart of the Baby Boomer generation.*

Some researchers conclude that individuals in the Leading Edge sub-cohort are more idealistic,[12] while Trailing Edge Boomers lean towards being more pragmatic.[13]

With those seemingly wide gaps in politics and popular culture noted, Baby Boomers overall share many common needs, goals, and perspectives. For example, most Baby Boomers share a deep concern for financial security, personal enrichment, and psychological growth. They also share an interest in maintaining optimal health and wellness. As a collective group, Baby Boomers often demonstrate a strong drive to make a real difference in society, assert themselves as meaningful members of their communities, and want to create a positive legacy for the world they will one day leave behind.

Retirees and Racial Diversity

Today's older population is less ethnically and racially diverse than the U.S. population as a whole. According to the most recent U.S. Census data in 2010, 64% of all Americans identified as white,[14] 13% reported African-American, and 16% percent reported Hispanic (Between 2000 and 2010, the Hispanic population grew 3% and represented over half of all U.S. population growth. I note this with a bit of irony as the author of a book about white Americans migrating to Mexico). According to the Federal Interagency Forum on Aging-Related Statistics,[15] Americans 65-years-old and older are about 78% white, 8.7% African-American, and 7.7% Hispanic. Racial distribution[16] for younger Baby Boomers is slightly more diverse than

---

[12] Green, 2005. Ibid.

[13] Green, 2005. Ibid.

[14] U.S. Census Bureau. (2011, March 24). 2010 Census shows America's Diversity.

[15] Federal Interagency Forum on Aging and Related Statistics. Older Americans 2016: Key indicators of Well-being.

[16] Colby & Ortman, 2014. Ibid.

that of their parents, with whites representing 72% of the cohort, African-Americans 11.6%, and Hispanics representing 10.5% of the Baby Boomer population. In later chapters, we will look at the racial distribution of the Mexico Boomers. You will learn that racial diversity is almost non-existent, with nearly 90% of all respondents reporting as white, about 8.5% reporting as Hispanic and only 0.3% reporting African American. (Yes, you read that correctly – I located only one African-American Mexico Boomer. It doesn't take much analysis to see that African Americans are underrepresented in Mexico when looking at the racial profile of American Baby Boomers as a whole. (Understanding the reasons will take a bit more room than I have left in this parenthesis but keep reading.)

Changing Baby Boomer Family Structure

One challenge for Baby Boomers to financing the traditional retirement model has been significant changes in the family structure. Baby Boomers are the children of the "nuclear family." For most, their mothers stayed home while their fathers went to work making a decent living and a nice pension. But at the turn of the 21st century, only 7% of American households represented this model.[17] As early as 2002, 87% of married couples reported that both spouses participated in the workforce.[18]

The institution of marriage continues to evolve. The percentage of the U.S. population who has never been married is rising. Today,[19] about 1 in 5 adults over the age of 25 have never been married. Compare that to 1 in 10 in 1960. And while the divorce rate has remained a steady 50% over the last 40 years, the

---

[17] Wilmoth, & Longino, 2006. Ibid.

[18] Wilmoth, & Longino, 2006. Ibid.

[19] Wang, W. & Parker, K. (2014, September 24). Record share of Americans have never married as values, economics and gender patterns change. *Pew Research Center.*

divorce rate for Baby Boomers is over 40%[20] higher than any other age group. According to the Washington Post,[21] "The Baby Boom generation was responsible for the extraordinary rise in marital instability after 1970. They are now middle-aged, but their pattern of high marital instability continues." In 2002, the U.S. Census Bureau reported that over 30% of Baby Boomers were unmarried. This is significant because individuals who are married generate significantly more wealth than individuals who are not.[22] This increased wealth is the result[23] of a number of factors, including dual incomes, joint assets, reduced costs for childcare and housing, capital appreciation, and home ownership. Married people[24] also have a larger proportion of disposable income, which can be used for reinvestment or to generate compound interest. The reduced number of marriages and dual-income households among Baby Boomers is sure to affect how and when they will retire and the financial resources available for it.

Female Retirees

Single women, who traditionally command lower salaries and fewer promotions than their male counterparts, are a growing demographic who will need new and inventive forms of retirement planning.[25] Some female Baby Boomers will be entering retirement

---

[20] Kennedy, S. & Ruggles, S. (2014). Breaking up is hard to count: The rise of divorce in the United States, 1980-2010. *Demography, 51*(2), 587-598.

[21] Ingraham, C. (2014, March 27). Divorce is actually on the rise, and it's the Baby Boomers' fault. *The Washington P*

[22] Wilmoth, J. & Koso, G. (2002). Does Marital History Matter? Marital Status and Wealth Outcomes Among Preretirement Adults. *Journal of Marriage and the Family, 64*, 254-268.

[23] Painter, M.A. (2008). The paths to marriage: Cohabitation and marital wealth accumulation.

[24] Painter, 2008. Ibid.

[25] Cohen, P. N., Huffman, M. L. & Knauer, S. (2009). Stalled Progress?: Gender Segregation and Wage Inequality Among Managers, 1980-2000. *Work and Occupations, 36*, 318-342.

with significant financial challenges, such as living five years longer than men on average, while having accumulated less wealth.[26] According to Street and Willmoth,[27] a smaller percentage of women than men receive occupational pensions. Further, women who do receive pensions usually receive lower amounts than men.[28] This occurs, in part, because although Baby Boomer women entered the workforce in higher numbers than women of the previous generation, they entered in a smaller percentage, entered later, and withdrew earlier than their male counterparts.[29] Additionally, in between positions women are more likely than men to have made early withdrawals from their retirement funds, thus suffering substantial tax penalties and a reduced fund for the long term.[30] Finally, women are more likely than men to experience downward financial mobility as a result of divorce,[31] another potential setback given that divorce rates among Baby Boomers are drastically higher than any other generation.

There is no doubt that Baby Boomers are a diverse generation spread over a very dynamic period in U.S. history. But as they enter retirement, they all share some very common and significant financial challenges. Before we start to explore those challenges in greater detail and determine the extent to which they motivate Baby Boomers to migrate to Mexico, let's first look at how

---

[26] National Vital Statistics Reports (2007). Deaths: Preliminary Data for 2007, 58(1).

[27] Street, D. & Wilmoth, J. (2001). Social Insecurity? Women and Pensions in the U.S. pp. 120-41 in J. Ginn, D. Street & S. Arber (Eds.) *Women, Work and Pensions: International Issues and Prospects*. Philadelphia: Open University Press.

[28] Street & Wilmoth, 2001. Ibid.

[29] Schieber, S. J. (1996). The Sleeping Giant Awakens: U.S. Retirement Policy in the 21st Century. *Compensation & Benefits Review, 28*, 20-31.

[30] Hass, W. H. & Serow, W. J. (2002). The Baby Boom, Amenity Retirement, Migration, and Retirement Communities: Will the Golden Age of Retirement Continue? *Research on Aging, 24(1)*,150-164.

[31] Newman, K.S. (1999). *Falling From Grace: The Experience of Downward Mobility in the American Middle Class*. New York: Free Press.

retirement was invented over 140 years ago, and what it looks like today.

In their own words...

In 1982, Jim and Iven met at a nightclub in Wichita, Kansas. Jim was 25, and Iven was 30.

Jim had gone to Baker University where he eventually earned an MBA and was working in advertising. Iven had just left his job as a telephone operator to purchase a flower shop and go into business for himself.

As two young gay men living in Kansas in the 1970s, Jim admits they spent a great deal of time "in the closet." But by 1985, they were out and open in their relationship and eventually became pillars of the Wichita social and business community. "When Iven and I realized we were serious about each other, we just decided to conduct our lives as if everyone already knew. We didn't flaunt it, but we didn't hide it either."

Before meeting Iven, Jim had never ventured out of the country. But with business success came the money to travel, and soon they were visiting places all over Mexico.

"We first became aware of San Miguel in the late 80s," Iven said. They had friends who would fondly reminisce about their time studying art at the Instituto Allende. But it wasn't until 2003 that they finally made a trip there for spring break. "It was like nowhere we had ever been," Jim said. "We knew within 3 days that we were going to retire there." They went home and started to work on a plan.

They had booked a return trip for December 29, 2005, but just a day before they were to leave, they were awoken by horrendous news. "It was around 2am and a friend called to say that there was smoke billowing from the flower shop," Iven said. "We rushed down there to arrive just after the fire department. From 3:00

to 6:00 a.m., we just sat in silence and watched my store burn to the ground." The fire was too large and lasted too long to save anything. "There was nothing left. There wasn't anything to salvage or rebuild," Iven said. "The fire marshal said we couldn't even enter the building, so we just decided to continue on with our scheduled trip to San Miguel and sort everything out when we got home."

While in San Miguel, Jim and Iven were shocked to learn the fire was arson. The police looked at it as a possible hate crime (though their main suspect would go on the run for 10 years before being caught and striking a plea deal for a lesser charge). They were also shocked to learn that rumors had started to circulate back home that Iven had started the fire in an effort to collect insurance money. "This was just incredible to me. I had been part of this community for 35 years and all of the sudden I felt like I was under the microscope," he said. "At first I was indignant. My gut reaction was to rebuild my store and my reputation, but at a point I just stopped. I realized this tragedy was really two-fold. First, the loss of my business, and second, the realization that I no longer knew who my friends were." That's when they decided they were done living in Kansas and to make their move to San Miguel as soon as possible.

By the time they arrived they were still only in their mid-50s. Though they had the financial means, they weren't really ready to retire. Iven managed a retail shop in the city, and Jim started working for a real estate company. They both caution that starting a business in Mexico isn't necessarily easy. "A lot of people who have been successful in the states are not successful here," Iven said, "They seem to have a real hard time letting go of what they're used to and settling in on the way things are done in Mexico." Iven admits he's one of those people. "People always ask me why I don't open another store," he says. "The answer is I'm just not patient enough to do business here. It's too different than what I'm used to. Products take longer to get. They are more expensive. You have to work longer hours to make less money." "Yes," Jim adds, "If people come down here and expect their income to be just like that in the U.S., but everything else to be cheaper, they're not going to make it."

34

Most expats in Mexico can't work because of residency restrictions. Jim explained. "A foreigner can't just come down here and get a work permit that takes a job from a Mexican. If you want to work, you have to get either temporary (4-year) or permanent residency status. That process can take four months to four years. To qualify, you have to prove that you won't be a burden on Mexico. That means showing you already have between $1500 and $2600 in monthly income. Once you have permanent residence status, you can work in Mexico without restrictions."

Both Jim and Iven have become permanent residents of Mexico. "I work just as many hours a week here as I did back in the U.S.," Jim said. "But the pace is slower, and I enjoy myself more. When I'm walking across the city square to appointments, I have to allow 20 extra minutes. I always run into someone I know. You have to stop and say hi. That's just the way we do it here."

Both Jim and Iven have had to make periodic trips back to the U.S. for different tasks. They each have a better perspective on the high-strung energy that permeates the United States. "You go back to the U.S., and you can instantly cut the stress in the air with a knife," Iven says. "There's so much anxiety. Everyone is in such a hurry. Nobody makes eye contact."

Both insist life in Mexico is better. "This has been such a fun adventure – it's not easy anywhere you go, but it's been a great, fun adventure for us," Jim explained. "People say Mexico either spits you out or embraces you. San Miguel just grabbed our hearts so hard we had no other choice but to live here," Iven added.

When asked if they'd ever return to the U.S., the answer is clear. "No, no, no," they said, both adamantly denying they'll ever go back. "If we wanted to move again, we'd move to another city in Mexico." But that doesn't mean they haven't worried about being forced out of the country.

"A few years ago, the day after Trump was elected, I was walking to my office when one of my good Mexican friends came up to me," Iven said. "He gave me a great big hug and said 'I'm sorry. I know it's not your fault.'" They both just laughed. "Luckily, we've never experienced any negativity or discrimination over being U.S. citizens in Mexico," Jim said. Iven nods in agreement and said with a smile, "We're on the fun side of the wall."

CHAPTER 3

A History of Retirement in the United States
Historical Perspective
Traditional Financing
When We Retire
Places and Communities

Here is a fun fact: Before 1960, our "Golden Years" did not even exist. The term "Golden Years" was actually coined in 1959 when it was used to sell homes in a brand new retirement community called Sun City.[1] Located in the heart of the Arizona desert, Sun City was one of the first large-scale 55+ "Active Retirement" communities launched in the United States. Today, most of us take for granted the idea that we need to go somewhere to retire. But just 50 to 60 years ago that concept was totally brand new and, like most tightly held beliefs about retirement, totally invented.

Today, a dynamic financial and employment landscape makes it a little harder to pinpoint what, exactly, retirement will look like for all of us. But even though we differ on how we'll actually do it, the present expectation for retirement sounds something like this: Work until you're 65 or 67. Make a voluntary withdrawal from the workforce. Collect your Social Security and retirement contributions. Sell the family home. Pocket some cash and downsize to a smaller

---

[1] Ramsey, D. Retirement revolution: How today's retirees are changing our concept of retirement.

place in a hip retirement community. Golf. Travel. Maybe volunteer. Have a heart attack in your sleep and die. Finally, cash in that funeral insurance. Memorial. Ground. Over.

I suppose for some of us that all sounds pretty good. But the fact that any of that was even an option is relatively new. In fact, the average life expectancy in the United States only hit 65 in 1942. By the "Golden Years" in 1960, it was up to about 69. Today, according to the World Bank, the current life expectancy of someone living in the U.S. is almost 79 years. So, since the first inhabitants moved to Sun City, we have added about 10 more years to our lives. Not bad. (If that's not good enough for you then you should have been born in Japan. They are number one in the world with a life expectancy of 83.7 years.)[2]

Getting old hasn't always been this easy. Retiring hasn't always been an option. Retirement rituals and practices related to old age have changed dramatically over time. During the Stone Age, retirement didn't exist because there weren't any old people. Just a little over half the population lived to be over 15 years old, with an average life expectancy of 33 years. According to Mary-Lou Weisman,[3] if someone made it past 30, that individual was probably worshipped and then eaten by others in the community as a sign of respect.

Weisman also notes that by the time of the Old Testament (let's call this 600-100 BC), a larger number of people were living into their 40s. Nonetheless, as they grew older, these elders did not stop working. Much like oxen, men and women alike were expected to work in some capacity until they keeled over and died. While the Old Testament includes tales of patriarchs living to be hundreds of years

---

[2] List of countries by life expectancy. (2019, December 3). *In Wikipedia.*

[3] Weisman, M.L. (1999, March 21). The history of retirement from early man to A.A.R.P. *The New York Times.*

old, God never asked any of them to stop working and move to Sun City.

In the late Middle Ages (1300-1500s), the population of older men and women increased dramatically. If you could survive childhood and the plague, you might actually make it to 60 years old![4] This was the first time older people posed an economic concern. While older women could be sent off to live in convents, the growing population of older men was quite problematic. Because fathers were taking so long to die, their property wasn't passing quickly enough to their sons. Fathers who lived longer spent more. So sons were forced to garner employment away from the home and stay in that work longer. While some sons took it all in stride, others simply killed their fathers as a means of achieving financial stability.

The concept of organized retirement in the colonies can be traced to Thomas Paine. In 1795, Paine,[5] the author of Common Sense and a forefather of the American Revolution, called for the "establishment of a public system of economic security for the new nation." He proposed a 10% inheritance tax that would be distributed to people over 50. While his plan never came to fruition, it does mark the beginning of the idea that government has a role to play in protecting older people against poverty.

While not a universal benefit for older folks, the aftermath of the Civil War (1861-1865) marked the largest government expenditure of benefits to citizens in the United States. By 1894, pension benefits for soldiers and widows comprised 37% of the entire federal budget.[6]

---

[4] Life Expectancy. (2019, December 11). *In Wikipedia.*

[5] Social Security Administration. Pre-social security period: Traditional sources of economic security.

[6] Social Security Administration. Ibid.

According to the U.S. Bureau of Labor Statistics,[7] American Express was the first company to offer an employee pension plan back in 1875. At that time,[8] American Express's primary business was mail service and money orders. The plan covered disabled employees over the age of 60 who had completed 20 years of service and had been recommended for retirement by a manager. Then, an executive committee of the board of directors had to approve the manager's recommendation for retirement benefits. Got it?

In 1880, the Baltimore and Ohio Railroad Company created the first employer/employee co-funded pension program in the United States, covering over 77,000 workers.

A few years later, and a continent away, German Chancellor Otto von Bismarck[9] made his nation the first to require retirement insurance. In 1889, Germany launched the world's first old-age social insurance system, funded through a combination of employee, employer, and government contributions. While everyone was required to pay in, benefits were only paid out if you made it to 70 years old, an unusual feat back in 1889, and a sure-fire way to keep the program from going bust.

At the beginning of the 20th century, the United States was experiencing a significant shift in the labor force as the country become further industrialized. How and when people retired depended on their occupations. In 1900, about 40% of the U.S. labor force was made up of farmers and agricultural workers (by 2002, it was less than 2%). Most people lived on the farms they worked, and family made up a majority of the labor force. Generally speaking, Americans who farmed did so late into their lives. When they were

---

[7] Seburn, P.W. (1991, December). Evolution of employer-provided defined benefit pensions. *Monthly Labor Review.*

[8] American Express. (2019, December 11). *In Wikipedia.*

[9] Social Security Administration. Otto van Bismarck, German Chancellor 1862-1890.

no longer able to work, their children took over the farm and cared for their parents. That cycle proved successful for a number of generations, until improved technology provided larger yields with the need for fewer workers, and somewhere off in the distance, a world war was raging that would displace hundreds of thousands of families.[10]

In the aftermath of World War I, the city was the new center of American life. Through the 1920s, the urban jungle became home to about 55% of the U.S. population (today it's over 80%). Long-gone was the call of the family farm. Metropolitan America promised riches beyond compare. "Old money" was displaced by a new world of entrepreneurs and industrial magnates. Stock markets and high finance promised a piece of the pie to almost anyone with cash. By 1928, large swaths of America believed easy fortunes could be made with brains over brawn. Then, in 1929, someone knocked the pie from the window sill. The Great Depression suffered 25% unemployment,[11] a stock market that had lost 80% of its value,[12] and the failure of nearly half of U.S. banks. After a decade of excess, Americans found themselves broke and out of work. They looked to their leaders for help. Their leaders created Social Security.

Traditional Retirement Financing

On August 14, 1935, President Franklin D. Roosevelt signed the Social Security Act,[13] creating our nation's first government-implemented retirement benefits program. In 1940,[14] the first cohort of eligible Americans started receiving monthly benefits (the first benefit paid was for $22.54). In 1940, a total of $35 million was paid

---

[10] World War I casualties. (2019, December 11). *In Wikipedia.*

[11] Great Depression. (2019, November 19). *In Wikipedia.*

[12] History.com. The stock market crash of 1929.

[13] Social Security Administration. Ibid.

[14] Social Security. (2019, December 9). *In Wikipedia.*

to 222,488 beneficiaries. By 2015,[15] Social Security comprised 24% of the federal budget and paid $888 billion in benefits to 40 million retired workers. Today, at least 50% of retired people 65 and older could not survive without it. According to AARP,[16] about 25% of retired persons 65 years old or older are almost entirely dependent on Social Security, and another 25% report that Social Security makes up a majority of their retirement income.

At its creation, Social Security was never meant to be a person's sole source of retirement income.[17] Rather, it was intended as a cornerstone of a larger retirement plan that included personal savings, private retirement funds, and pensions.

Unlike Social Security, the Great Depression did not launch the pension plan as we know it. From 1875 to 1929, 421 private sector pension plans were already established. At the start of the Great Depression, about 400 still existed. In 1940, when Roosevelt's Social Security program started paying out regular monthly benefits, 15% of private-sector workers were also eligible for some sort of pension. By 1950, 25% of all private-sector workers were covered by a pension plan. By 1960 that figure had jumped to over 40%. The year 1980 may represent the pinnacle of the traditional pension plan, in which 46% of all private-sector workers were covered.

In a traditional pension plan, a specific amount of monthly income is guaranteed by the plan provider, say General Motors (GM). This is called a "defined benefit plan." It's up to GM to define the benefit and appropriately invest or store retirement funds so they can be paid out in accordance with the plan. If GM fails to do so, the

---

[15] Center on Budget and Policy Priorities. (2019, January 29). Policy basics: Where do our federal tax dollars go?

[16] Caldera, S. (2012). Social Security: Who's counting on it? AARP Public Policy Institute.

[17] Caldera, S. (2012). Ibid.

company is still on the hook for the retirement money they promised to their retired workers and has to find a way to pay it (sometimes from current profits). But in the 1980s, the defined benefit plan started to be replaced with the "defined contribution plan."

Today, defined contribution plans make up a majority of retirement funds. In a defined contribution plan, such as the 401(k), income is not guaranteed. Rather than company managers, employees make the decisions about where their retirement funds are invested. They also assume all of the risk. The rationale behind this shift from traditional pensions to the 401(k) is that the defined contribution plan gives employees more control over their retirement planning and the freedom to choose the investments they want to make. That is great if, in addition to working as an auto plant laborer, you are also a stock market expert. But it is not so great if you have no idea what you are investing in and the market underperforms. It is even worse if a majority of your 401(k) is made up of your company's stock at a time when your company decides to participate in risky or "aggressive" investment strategies. At the time of the 2008 financial crisis, those on the cusp of retirement lost anywhere between 20-35% of their retirement funds.[18] Some reported losing even more.[19] While younger investors may still have time to recover, these were catastrophic losses for Baby Boomers who were scheduled to retire just five years later at a rate of 10,000 a day.[20]

---

[18] Employee Benefit Research Institute.

[19] CBS News. (2009, April 17). Retirement dreams disappear with 401(k)s.

[20] Friedberg, B.A. (2019, September 23). Are we in a Baby Boomer retirement crisis? *Investopedia.*

When We Retire

According to Wilmoth and Longino,[21] over the past 50 years the age of retirement for men and women has declined dramatically in the United States. The U.S. Bureau of Labor and Statistics (2001) reported that in 1950, the average retirement age of men was 68.5 years old and 67.9 years old for women. By 2000, the average age of retirement for men had dropped to 62.6 and to 62.5 for women.[22] In 2019,[23] the average age of retirement had crept up to 64 for men and fallen to 62 for women. Economists disagree as to whether these trends will continue. Some predict an increase in retirement age due to changes in Social Security policy.[24] Earlier researchers[25] believed early retirement would remain an affordable option.

With increases in life expectancy,[26] the retirement phase is currently predicted to represent 24% of a person's life,[27] another big change that sets Boomers apart from their parents' generation.

Where Baby Boomers Go to Retire

Retired Leading Edge Boomers are starting to reveal some trends about how Boomers retire. According to the U.S. Census Bureau,[28] Leading Edge Baby Boomers are migrating in significant

---

[21] Wilmoth, & Longino, 2006. Ibid.

[22] (Glendell 2001).

[23] Kurt, D. (2019, November 25). 'When should I retire?' The pros and cons of different ages. *Investopedia.*

[24] Clark, R. & Quinn, J. (2002). Patterns of Work and Retirement for a New Century, *Generations* 26(2), 17-24.

[25] Costa, D. (1998). *The Evolution of Retirement.* Chicago: University of Chicago Press.

[26] Centers for Disease Control and Prevention, National Vital Statistics Reports (2004). Table 12. Estimated Life Expectancy at Birth in Years, by Race and Sex."

[27] Wilmoth, & Longino, 2006. Ibid.

[28] Sightings, T. (2015, March 30). Where retirees want to live now. *U.S. News. & World Report.*

numbers to the Sun Belt. This includes both permanent residence and snowbirds who flock there seasonally.

Of the 20 most rapidly growing communities in the United States, six are located in Florida. Over the last five years[29] the fastest growing metropolitan area in the United States is The Villages, a city an hour north of Orlando.[30] The Villages[31] (which brands itself "Florida's Friendliest Retirement Hometown") is a retirement community whose environment is appealing to many Boomers. Large communities of this nature include single family residences, townhomes, and condominiums. Communities like The Villages provide a variety of recreational options. For just one day in December 2019, the Village's event calendar offered club meetings or gatherings related to tennis, quilting, sewing, golf, bocce ball, movies, astronomy, home brewing, stamp collecting, cards, canoeing, investing, swimming, painting, archery, computers, cooking, and dancing, just to name a few![32] These types of retirement communities also usually feature fitness centers, dining, and transportation options. And an increasing number are now offering onsite doctor's offices.

Baby Boomers have acquired a second moniker that could dramatically impact where they retire: the Sandwich Generation.[33] Some Baby Boomers find themselves in the middle of providing a home to their children and also their parents. In increasing numbers,[34] children are living with their Boomer parents longer. Some of this has been blamed on a poor job market for college graduates. In fact, one-third of all college students say they plan to

---

[29] Sauter, M.B. (2016, April 4). America's fastest growing cities. 247WallSt.com

[30] Sightings, 2005. Ibid.

[31] TheVillages.com

[32] TheVillages.com

[33] ABC News. (2006, January 6). Baby Boomers supporting kids and parents.

[34] Byrne, J.A. (2016, May 14). College grads are moving home for help from mom and dad. *New York Post.*

live with their parents after graduation.[35] While unemployment figures have gone down over the last several years, these numbers say little about the quality of the jobs available.[36] College graduates may take low paying service jobs to make ends meet, and while they're saddled with record student loans,[37] it may be some time before they are able to afford housing on their own. As for "The Greatest Generation," they too are finding that rising housing and medical costs are making it impossible to survive without some assistance from their adult children.[38] Even if Boomers are not providing housing to their parents, they may be providing at least some financial support. In fact, according to AARP, 48% of Baby Boomers thought they should be doing more for their parents.[39]

An emerging trend among a small, yet growing, number of Baby Boomers is cohabitation. Unrelated Baby Boomers are actively seeking one another out to share a home and expenses.[40] There are a number of websites dedicated to shared living, including www.GoldenGirlsNetwork.com, www.NationalSharedHousing.org, and www.SeniorsHomeExchange.com (none of which I endorse or recommend. I'm simply providing these links for reference). The shared housing concept satisfies a number of needs for retired persons, including reduced costs, safety and security, and a sense of community. It's also an alternative for folks who are not looking for the size and structure of retirement communities like The Villages.

---

[35] Eiger, M. & Schiavone, J. (2015, November 12). One-third of college students say they'll live at home post-graduation due to loan debt. *AICPA.org*.

[36] Morath, E. (2014, June 9). Jobs return to peak, but quality lags. *The Wall Street Journal*.

[37] Mitchell, J. (2016, May 2). Student debt is about to set another record, but the picture isn't all bad. *The Wall Street Journal*.

[38] Hoak, A. (2014, November 22). More parents move in with their kids. *MarketWatch*.

[39] ABC News, 2006. Ibid.

[40] Mears, T. (2015, April 20). How Baby Boomers are creating their own retirement communities. *U.S. News and World Report*.

These traditional and evolving retirement settings are part of a new trend that includes Baby Boomers venturing across borders and into foreign lands. While we've touched on some of the challenges related to retirees in general, it's time we dig deep into the finances of Baby Boomers to uncover how, exactly, money might motivate them to leave the United States.

In their own words...

Richard grew up in a tight-knit, all-American home in Philadelphia. His father was a World War II veteran and his entire family were self-proclaimed "flag-wavers." "For every American holiday," Richard said, "we were going out decorating graves with American flags for veterans. We had an 18-foot flagpole on our front lawn. I did a formal flag ceremony in my Boy Scouts uniform every day."

Fresh out of college, Richard decided to join his father in their long-standing family flooring business. Richard's father begged him to consider another career path, but Richard was adamant. He was very good at the business, and a few years after joining, his father handed it down to him. The operation was successful for a little while, until a difficult divorce forced him to dissolve the company and start taking work as a subcontractor.

At 36-years-old, Richard was newly remarried when he suffered a devastating heart attack that required bypass surgery. The doctors warned him about a return to physical work. Eventually, he took a position in sales with another Philadelphia flooring company, thinking office work would be far less strenuous. "I was wrong," he said, "This position was much more turbulent and high-pressure than any other work environment I've been in." On top of this, Richard was served with a second divorce. "It was such a stressful time, and then, one day I blacked out and woke up in the hospital." Richard had another heart attack. This time, instead of being told to take it easy, he was told he had about six months to live. "Three out of the four cardiologists I met with told me my heart was too weak to go on much longer. That was terrifying."

Richard took stock of his situation and decided to stop working and move in with his mother. His own condition stabilized, but his mother's health began to fail. Between all of his own and his mother's health care issues, Richard met and began dating a nurse, Karen. The two fell in love fast, but shortly after they were married Richard's mom passed away. At that point, Richard and Karen decided to move into a 55+ community in Fort Myers, Florida.

"Shortly after the move, I had back surgery, and I was laid up for about a month," Richard said. "Karen took off from work to take care of me. Even though I was in pain and grumpy, we were having a really great time together, just talking and relaxing."

The two of them began discussing ways to spend even more free time together, but Karen was too young for retirement benefits, and Richard's pension was too small to support them both.

"Karen started looking online for other parts of the country where our cost of living would be lower," Richard says. "And then she stumbled on the country of Belize." They had not considered moving out of the U.S., but intrigued, they took a two-week vacation to the town of Corozal. "The reality wasn't quite as promising as the advertisements," Richard lamented. "It reminded me of some bombed out cities from WWII. Some of the houses didn't have windows or roofs. None of the roads were paved. We were very unhappy, very disillusioned there; it was nothing like we had read about."

They did, however, meet a Canadian couple who were in Belize for work. Karen explained they were looking for a cheap place to retire, and the Canadians suggested they visit Playa del Carmen. Richard promptly cancelled their existing reservations and booked the first flight out of Belize to Mexico. "We checked out the cost of living," he said. "We could rent a place in town, close to a doctor and a pharmacy." They put pen to paper. "From what we calculated, it seemed like we could live there just on my pension — it would be a little tight and a little rough, but we could do it."

In the end, they settled on the town of Mérida, and returned home to make their own 5-year-plan to move there. But within a few months, Hurricane Irma landed *in their retirement community, ravaging a lot of the homes. "We were fortunate — we had very little damage, but it became clear it was time for us to move." Karen was also in a good position to leave. She had left nursing for a job processing insurance claims from home, over the phone — a job she could theoretically do from anywhere. By October 2017, the couple were living in Mexico full-time.*

Richard describes his final months in the U.S., just after Donald Trump's inauguration and while everyone else around him seemed to be discussing leaving America. "In the very beginning, I kind of felt guilty, like I was betraying my country. I didn't want anyone to think we were running from something." But even with unwavering love for his homeland, he was equally frustrated that the U.S. healthcare system made it impossible for him to live there. "Medical expenses continued to gouge our savings. Medicare doesn't cover many of my issues. Most of Karen's salary was going to copays. In the end, it wasn't that we were running from something, we were just trying to find a place, any place, that we could afford."

Today, the couple is comfortable in their new home in Mérida. Richard's pension of $1,800 per month covers a three-bedroom house with two-and-a-half baths, a small yard and patio, an enclosed carport, and a swimming pool. They have been able to budget for a housekeeper and for someone to care for the pool a couple of times per week. When medical issues do arise, the amount they pay out of pocket in Mérida is still less than the copays back in the U.S.

Richard and Karen both agree that life is better for them in Mexico. "Mérida is clean and safe," Richard says. "The people are polite and kindhearted. And the town is alive with cultural events almost every night. I am very much impressed with the life we have found here in Mexico." Though Richard admits there are some places and people he misses very much back in the States, he insisted, "No, if given the chance to move back to the U.S., I would still want to stay right here, and I know Karen feels the same way."

CHAPTER 4

A Financial Profile of U.S. Baby Boomers
        Savings
        Retirement Funding
        Home Ownership
        Debt
        Current Finances of Baby Boomers

The U.S. Bureau of Labor Statistics regularly conducts the Consumer Expenditure Survey (CES). The CES estimates what different households spend on basic necessities. The CES estimates that the average retirement household (which it designates as two people) spends $40,938 annually.[1] Though it varies, let's call the average length of retirement in the United States 18 years. If we were to assume absolutely no increase in the cost of living (and if you promised to die right on time), the amount of money a household would require for retirement would be almost $737,000. If you want to get technical and include the stingy 1%-3% average annual cost of living increases Social Security provides, then that total comes to well over $750,000.

---

[1] Brandon, E. (2014, November 3). The high costs of the retirement dream. *U.S. News and World Report*.

Housing represents the largest expense for retired Baby Boomers averaging $14,034 per year.[2] Annual transportation costs average $6,651, while food eats up another $5,126 of the budget. Out-of-pocket healthcare and medical expenses cost an average of $5,094.[3] Entertainment, clothing, and personal care consume the rest.

With 18 years of retirement barreling down on Baby Boomers, at a cost of $750,000, understanding how prepared they are to meet those financial challenges might explain why they are motivated to consider retirement in Mexico.

Baby Boomer Retirement Savings

According to a recent survey by the Insured Retirement Institute (IRI), 45% of Baby Boomers have saved absolutely nothing for retirement.[4] Nineteen percent claimed to have at least $250,000 in retirement funds. About 20% said that financial difficulties over the last year have made it impossible to continue to contribute to their existing retirement accounts. And nearly 30% think they will need to work into their 70s to make ends meet. Based on these results, at a minimum, 4 out of 5 Baby Boomers are nowhere near ready to meet the financial challenges of traditional retirement in the U.S. While the survey notes that a majority of Baby Boomers remain optimistic about their ability to make up the difference, the Institute writes, "These Boomers likely have unrealistic retirement expectations, based on the current state of economic affairs in the United States."

In addition to what Baby Boomers report about themselves, economists and social scientists have been following these financial

---

[2] Brandon, 2014. Ibid.

[3] Brandon, 2014. Ibid.

[4] Weil, D. (2015, April 16). Survey: 40 percent of Baby Boomers haven't saved for retirement. *NewsMax*.

developments with more thorough investigations. Studies related to Baby Boomers' personal finances find that only 57% have retirement accounts, with a median amount of $2000 in them.[5] According to Hass and Serow, 401(k) retirement plans have overly exposed Baby Boomer retirement accounts to fluctuations in the market, forcing Baby Boomers to work longer to accumulate the same retirement savings as their parents.[6] A 2010 Gallup poll[7] found that over one-third of Americans are expecting to rely on Social Security as a major retirement funding source. This might not be a wise plan given that there is no consensus on how long Social Security will last, or when, if, and how much payouts may decline.[8] Reduced retirement funds are also due, in part, to rising health care and prescription drug costs, which have at least doubled the rate of inflation over the last 30 years.[9] Rising healthcare costs are also increasing the strain on entitlement programs such as Medicaid and Medicare – costs that are expected to increase dramatically over the next 20 years.[10] Finally, AARP reports that more than half of all Boomers believe they will never save enough money to be able to retire, a self-assessment that may be spot on.[11]

---

[5] DeVaney, S. A. & Chiremba, S. T. (2005). Comparing the Retirement Savings of the Baby Boomers and Other Cohorts. *United States Department of Labor. Bureau of Labor and Statistics.*

[6] Hass & Serow, 2002. Ibid.

[7] Gallup. (2010). Americans Shift Expectations About Retirement Funding.

[8] Social Security Administration (2011). *Proposals Addressing Trust Fund Solvency.*

[9] Basu 2005:29

[10] Truffer, C. (February 2010). Health Spending Projections Through 2019: The Recession's Impact Continues. *Health Affairs.*

[11] Huffman, M. (2019, September 9). New survey of Baby Boomers shows mounting retirement challenges. *Consumer Affairs.*

Financing Retirement: How Baby Boomers Will Fund Their Golden Years

As stated in earlier chapters, the first wave of Leading Edge Baby Boomers have retired. What we know so far is that they appear to be relying heavily upon Social Security to fund their retirement. Thirty-seven percent of Leading Edge Boomers rely primarily on Social Security to pay for retirement, while 19% are dependent upon pensions. Only 11% are utilizing their own savings and private investments as primary means of retirement funding.[12] Nearly one-third of Leading Edge Baby Boomer retirees continue to work past retirement age, with two-thirds of them still working full-time.

It remains to be seen how Trailing Edge Baby Boomers will fund their retirement.[13] A large section of that sub-cohort has yet to retire. However, survey data suggest that more of them will be relying solely on Social Security, and few will derive income from pensions. While some Trailing Edge Boomers might still have 10 years to work it out, most will be starting this home stretch with nothing. If they are going to generate the $750,000 needed to comfortably retire, they are going to have to create some financial innovations unmatched in the past. If they cannot raise those funds, then they will have to work much longer than their parents or find new ways to cut costs and reduce spending. A Mexican retirement may be one strategy that does that.

Baby Boomer Home Ownership

For many of us, homeownership is not just about having a place to hang our hats; it is also an investment. We expect our home

---

[12] Sightings, 2014. Ibid.
[13] Sightings, 2014. Ibid.

values to slowly rise year-over-year and to one day sell those homes to help fund our Golden Years. But is that still a realistic expectation?

Overall, homeownership is down in the United States, from its peak of 69% in 2004 to about 63% today.[14] According to the U.S. Bureau of Labor Statistics, between 2000 and 2004 Trailing Edge Baby Boomer home ownership peaked at around 73%.[15] During the 2008 housing collapse, 7% of these homeowners were forced into foreclosure.

A study by the Joint Center for Housing Studies at Harvard University reveals that older Americans, including Baby Boomers from both sub-cohorts, are renting at higher rates than their predecessors. In fact, people from their late 40s into their mid-60s account for twice the share in residential rental demand than people under 35. Over the next few years, Baby Boomers are expected to represent half of all rental demand growth.

Unlike their parents, Baby Boomers tend to upgrade their homes. Rather than stay put, pay off an existing residence, and accumulate increased equity along the way, Boomers have preferred to move up to larger homes. The Census Bureau reports that from the 1960s through the end of the 20th century the average home size has steadily increased.[16] It was the Baby Boomer generation that drove the construction of giant, 2500+ square-foot homes that now dominate suburban communities from coast to coast.

Many Baby Boomers purchased their homes in the 1980s and 1990s and then enjoyed a fairly well sustained real estate market.[17] But many also upgraded to new homes before the 2008 housing

---

[14] U.S. Census Bureau. (2019, October 29). Quarterly residential vacancies and homeownership, third quarter 2019.

[15] Aughinbaugh, A. (2013 February). Patterns of homeownership, delinquency, and foreclosure among youngest Baby Boomers. *Special Studies & Research, 2*(2).

[16] Meehan, M. (2014, February 21). The Baby Boomer housing bust. *Forbes.*

[17] Meehan, 2014. Ibid.

crisis. Those who did may have lost significant equity as the bubble burst. Their homes may not be able to provide the cash needed to fund their post-retirement plans.

Simple supply and demand may be another reason why Baby Boomer home investments may go bust. Fannie Mae warns large numbers of retiring Boomers moving from single-family homes to apartments "could put downward pressure on single-family home prices."[18] The sizable number of Baby Boomer homes about to go on the market may far exceed Millennial demand. Generation X (myself included) has largely settled into their homes, and as shown in earlier chapters, Millennials may not be able to afford to buy for some time. Compounding the problem, multi-generational housing is on the rise and may be the new normal. According the Pew Research Center, nearly one in five young adults share a home with their parents, nearly double the rate in the 1980s.[19] This may simply be the temporary effect of tough economic times or a long-term solution for both Millennials and Baby Boomers who took on far too much debt (in both student loans and home mortgages). Whatever the case, lower demand will undoubtedly be driving down home prices into the next decade. Baby Boomers banking on their homes to help fund their retirement may need to reconsider.

Baby Boomer Debt

According to the New York Federal Reserve, debt held by Americans aged 50-80 increased by 59% from 2003 to 2015.[20] The Wall Street Journal reports that 65-year-olds today have 47% more

---

[18] Fannie Mae. (2015, August 19). Baby Boomer downsizing revisited: Boomers are not leaving their single-family homes for apartments. *Fannie Mae Housing Insights, 5*(2).

[19] Fry, R. & Passel, J.S. (2014, July 17). In post-recession era, young adults drive continuing rise in multi-generational living. *Pew Research Center*.

[20] Haughwout, A. (2016). Household debt and credit: 2015 in review. *Federal Reserve Bank of New York*.

mortgage debt and 29% more auto debt than 65-year-olds had in 2003.[21] Perhaps most interesting is older Americans' exploding student loan debt. Student loan debt for 65-year-olds rose a whopping 886% between 2003 and 2015.[22] It is not just their own student loan debt they are paying down – it is their children's as well.[23] This increase in Baby Boomer debt only seems to be accelerating over time.

If there is some good news about Baby Boomer debt, it is that Baby Boomers may be in the best position to pay it down. Older professionals bring home higher salaries, and in most cases, have accumulated assets to borrow against. The bad news is that if those assets include investments and homes earmarked for retirement, that first sell-off wave will be going to creditors rather than long-term care. If the amount Baby Boomers owe continues to rocket, we may all be in for a real shock as even the best heeled of the cohort concede they are broke.

In the end, painting a singular picture of Baby Boomer finances is a tricky endeavor. While the Leading Edge has retired, the Trailing Edge still has the next 10-12 years to change their trajectory. But 12 years is a long time. In addition to their own planning, they still face plenty of exposure to ongoing economic and housing booms and busts. Good timing may prove beneficial to some, good luck to others. Those who hold onto homes and other assets too long may pay a stiff price, while others may be well served to quickly sell and cut their losses. Whatever the outcome, one thing seems obvious: The traditional retirement model will be unattainable for a majority of Baby Boomers. To live comfortably into their later years, they will

---

[21] Zumbrun, J. (2016, February, 12). People over 50 carrying more debt than in the past. *The Wall Street Journal.*

[22] Durden, T. (2016, February 12). Baby Boomers are drowning in loans: Debt of average 67-year-old soared 169% in past 12 years. *ZeroHedge.*

[23] Fisher, A. (2016, May 6). Student debt is derailing Boomers' retirement. *Fortune.*

need to consider a combination of working longer, staying healthy, having smaller homes, cohabitating with family members, sharing a house with other retirees, stop buying new cars, paying off debt, revising disposable income expectations, and retiring in a country with a much lower cost of living.

In their own words...

Kerry grew up in Minnesota where everything was white: the landscape, the food, even all the people in her neighborhood. "Luckily my father, for all his faults, was a daredevil," she said. "He took me on his many escapades." She remembers being barely a toddler, holding onto his waist with her tiny arms as they zipped through traffic on his motorcycle. "We chased fire trucks and ambulances," she laughed. "I must have inherited his wild spirit since I spent so much of my adult life testing and checking boundaries."

Kerry's first experience with anything Spanish came during a high school trip she took to Spain. "I fell in love with the rich colors and flavors of the country," she remembers. "A few years later, in my twenties, I visited Mexico. I knew right away that Mexico was my destiny."

When she got older, she earned an MBA, "Which was unusual for women back then," she says. She worked in high tech and lived mostly in Texas, with one stint in Silicon Valley. "Work allowed me to travel the world and indulge in my crazy hobbies like track cars (I was even a Porsche Club instructor), scuba diving, and endurance horse racing."

Ironically, it was as a new MBA that she learned the "Parable of the Fisherman." "It's the story of a smug MBA who encounters a fisherman living a subsistence life fishing a few hours a day, laying in his hammock, and romancing his wife," she explained. "The MBA analyzes the situation and explains to the fisherman how much money he could make if he would just work his ass off for 25 years building a fishing empire. "And what could I do with all that money?" the fisherman asks? The MBA answers, "You wouldn't have to do anything. You could retire, fish for a few hours a day, lay in your hammock, and romance your wife. Wouldn't that be great?" This tale always stuck with me, yet I could never just let go and trust the universe enough to live a subsistence life. Instead I *worked my ass off for 25 years building my own little empire and running my own business so I could retire a little bit younger than everyone else."*

Kerry spent her whole adult life returning to Mexico. She visited every chance she could, most vacations and holidays. Around 2005, she had moved into technical writing and began coming down to Mexico to "finish a book." "This is when I discovered the Lake Chapala area," she said. "Only 12 hours from my Austin, Texas base, yet a world apart. The first time I drove up the winding mountain and looked down on the lake town below, it was love at first sight."

Over the next few years, she lived in various towns around the lake. She brought her endurance horse with her and explored the lakeshore and mountains for many hours and days. She even rode with a machete to hack away the jungle underbrush.

Over the years, she wrote 13 technical books from Chapala, spending 6 months to 2 years living in the area each time. Finally, she made the break for good and retired. "I bought a home in Chapala and renovated it. I have nearly all Mexican neighbors and speak Spanish most of the time."

Reflecting now, Kerry has no regrets, but said, "I wish I had had the courage to get here sooner, but life kept getting in the way. I wake up every day in paradise and have to pinch myself because my vacation never ends." Her horse is old now, but still with her and they ride every day. "I am grateful to Mexico and feel cradled in her arms," she said. "This country teaches me something about myself every day and keeps me humble."

PART II.

WHY WOULD ANYONE WANT TO LEAVE THE UNITED STATES?

CHAPTER 5

A History of Migration out of the United States

> Retiree Migration
>
> Late-life Migration
>
> U.S. Retirees in Mexico
>
> Websites, Television, Books and More

This entire book was inspired by trying to answer one question: *Why would anyone want to leave the United States?*

A History of Out-Migration

According to the U.S. Department of Homeland Security, millions of foreign nationals are involved in the immigration process – legally and illegally – every year. Although it is U.S.-bound migration that garners the most media attention, a slower flow of U.S. nationals is out-migrating (or emigrating) to other countries around the globe, including Mexico. As of 2014, there are an estimated 8.7 million U.S. citizens residing overseas. It is believed that one million of these expats live in Mexico,[1] however, counting the number of Americans living overseas is inexact.[2] Unlike other nations, the U.S. does not require its citizens – whether in country or abroad – to register a place of residence.

---

[1] International Living. One million Americans in Mexico can't all be wrong.

[2] Costanzo, J., Klekowski von Koppenfels, A. (2013, May 17). Counting the uncountable: Overseas Americans. *Migration Policy Institute.*

The freedom to move, including the ability to migrate from one jurisdiction to another, is enshrined in the Constitution of the United States, in what is known as the Privileges and Immunities Clause. The U.S. Supreme Court recognized that freedom of movement and travel is a fundamental right.[3]

During the post-colonial period, the freedom to travel and relocate mostly focused on movement between states. But now the focus is international. Provided that a U.S. citizen has a valid passport and is able to obtain an appropriate visa from a foreign country, individuals face few restrictions from visiting or even residing in another nation. The U.S. State Department does issue destination-specific warnings from time-to-time, when a particular foreign destination is deemed dangerous, but very rarely outright blocks international travel (though host country requirements and the unavailability of traditional commercial carriers may make some destinations seem impossible).

Perhaps the best-known travel and residency restriction ever placed on U.S. citizens involved the 50+ year, comprehensive embargo of Cuba.[4] Over the last 10 years, restrictions have started to ease. In 2015, relations with the Caribbean nation were normalized. Today, it is fairly easy to travel to Cuba, with regularly available commercial flights leaving from Miami.[5] What once was a serious matter for Baby Boomers, the Cuban travel ban will be nothing but a page in history books to future generations.

As far as Mexico is concerned, the U.S. government has never embargoed travel or emigration to the country. But restrictions did exist during the U.S.-Mexican War, fought from 1846 to 1848.

---

[3] Justia: U.S. Supreme Court. Paul v. Virginia, 75 U.S. 168 (1869).

[4] Suddath, C. (2009, April 15). A brief history of U.S.-Cuba Relations. *Time.*

[5] Satchell, A. (2016, September 7). American Airlines launches first flights to Cuba from Miami since 1961. *South Florida Sun Sentinel.*

And constant warnings about U.S. travel and residency in Mexico have been in place in certain parts of that nation over the last 25 years. These warnings have arisen out of concern about the narco wars and resulting drug cartel violence. While Americans are very rarely the targets of this violence, there is the possibility of being accidently caught in the middle of it – a concern that also exists in U.S. cities.

While Mexico is certainly the number one destination for U.S. expats, the rest of Latin America and the Caribbean are home to nearly a third of all U.S. citizens living abroad.[6] Only 20% of U.S. expats reside in Europe. The remaining balance are scattered in other locales around the globe, including Canada, Israel, the United Kingdom, Germany, and France.[7]

It is important to note that not all emigrants are retirees. North Americans elect to live abroad for many different reasons, including employment, education, family ties, marriage, and for some, adventure.

In his book Leaving America: The New Expatriate Generation, John R. Wennersten uncovers some obvious and not-so-obvious motivations for expatriation. The obvious include tax advantages, exotic self-indulgence, military service, and attractive corporate salaries. The not-so-obvious are far more interesting. Based on his own research, he identified six additional motivators that explain contemporary expatriate out-migration: (1) Transnational and Lifestyle Realization, (2) Cultural Dissonance, (3) Entrepreneurial Advancement, (4) Settlement and Re-adaptation, (5) Economic Dissent, and (6) Expanding Gender Domains.[8] A number of these

---

[6] Rice, M. (2010, June 4). Not everyone wants to live in America. *Forbes*.

[7] Costanzo & Klekowski von Koppenfels, 2013. Ibid.

[8] Wennersten, J.R. (2008). *Leaving America. The New Expatriate Generation*. Praeger. Westport, Connecticut.

motivations deserve a brief explanation, as they become very applicable to the research findings revealed later in this book.

Wennersten describes Transnational and Lifestyle Realization as a consequence of increasingly insignificant national borders and low costs of living that can allow for people of modest means to live abroad. Wennersten writes that, "For many people the goal is to find personal and economic freedom somewhere in the world and thereby escape the restrictions in their own society."

He explains Cultural Dissonance as "a symbolic melodrama in which many Americans are rejecting a conforming dream of a richer and fuller life that has drawn tens of millions of immigrants to our shores." He finds this motivation most pronounced in people who feel uncertain about what it means to be an American, feel American culture is much more fragmented than in the past, or have a loose historical memory and national consciousness.

Wennersten explains the motive of Entrepreneurial Advancement as mostly a migration phenomenon among young Americans who are taking advantage of "the openness of Eastern Europe and parts of Asia to free enterprise capitalism without the restrictions of age and experience that have traditionally hampered young people in America."

Wennersten explains Settlement and Re-adaptation as a movement by a significant number of foreign-born U.S. emigrants back to their home countries after having achieved economic success in the United States.

Wennersten explains the motivation of Economic Dissent as the avoidance of taxes in the U.S. or as taking advantage of more lenient foreign tax legislation.

Wennersten explains Expanding Gender Domains as primarily a migration motivator for women who feel that living abroad can transform traditional gender roles and expectations for women.

Now that we have some understanding of why people migrate out of the United States in general, let's explore why retirees specifically might feel compelled to do so.

Retiree Migration

There is evidence that some retirees do not trust U.S. policymakers to guarantee a comfortable retirement. According to AARP,[9] a growing number of U.S. retirees (currently 5%) are taking advantage of permanent international migration as one way to stretch their retirement dollars. Since 2008, AARP has published at least 15 separate reports or bulletins on U.S. Retiree migration into Mexico,[10] naming Puerto Vallarta as the best Mexican destination, citing its low cost of living and laid-back lifestyle as the area's primary attractions. But academic research about where these U.S. retirees are migrating to and what features they look for in destinations are scarce. It is surprising that researchers have been so slow to explore these questions, especially since businesses have not. A 2019 Google search for the keyword "international retirement" returns over 363 million relevant pages, with most of these first page results coming from international relocation 'experts', authors, and real estate agents. There is little in the academic literature addressing international retirement migration. Rather, researchers seem more concerned with exploring strategies for successful assimilation of U.S. business

---

[9] AARP 1999. Ibid.

[10] AARP. (2010). Mexico: First-class urban amenities and charming palm-fringed villages draw retirees to the Puerto Vallarta region.

people into foreign territories as U.S.-based corporations move into emerging economies.[111213]

Late-Life Migration

Migration late in life usually comes with a number of significant challenges. The psychological and physical impact of late-life migration is more severe compared to migrants who move earlier in the course of their lives.[14] Studies of elderly migrants moving into the United States show gaps in the availability of financial services, healthcare, and physical assistance as well as language barriers and an understanding of cultural norms.[15] Migration is also a mentally stressful time for seniors and requires strong social and familial support to decrease the chance of poverty and isolation.[16] Thus, the availability of family is the strongest incentive for late-life migration.[17] Senior migrants with inadequate social support tend to suffer poorer health than senior migrants with ample social support.[18] For migrants moving into the United States, ethnic enclaves provide economic and social support, which increases the chance of a successful migration.[19]

---

[11] Boyacigiller, N.A. (1989). The New Expatriates: Managing Human Resources Abroad. *Journal of International Business Studies, 20*(2), p. 361.

[12] Luthans, K.W. & Farner, S. (2002). Expatriate development: the use of 360-degree feedback. *Journal of Management Development, 21*(10).

[13] Gerrard, M.M. (2011). Global assignment effectiveness and leader development. *Advances in Global Leadership, 6.*

[14] Angel & Angel 1992:496.

[15] Garcia, J.L. (1985). A Needs Assessment of Elderly Hispanics in an Inner City Senior Citizen Complex: Implications for Practice. *Journal of Applied Gerontology, 4*(1), 72-85.

[16] Angel & Angel 1992. Ibid.

[17] Schmink, M. (1984). Household economic strategies: Review and Research Agenda. *Latin American Research Review, 19.* 87-101.

[18] House, J. S., Landis, K. R. & Umberson, D. (1988). Social Relationships and Health. *Science, 241,* 540-545.

[19] Portes, A., & Jensen, L. (1989). The enclave and the entrants: Patterns of ethnic enterprise in Miami before and after Mariel. *American Sociological Review, 54.* 929-949

Dr. David Truly provides the most comprehensive research on seniors migrating into Mexico. In 2002, Truly published *International retirement migration and tourism along the Lake Chapala Riveria: developing a matrix of retirement migration behavior.*[20] The purpose of this research was to identify motivations of U.S. retirees living in Lake Chapala, Mexico. Truly first identifies a number of reported historical motivators for retirement migration into the Lake Chapala region. These include wanting a tolerant, egalitarian, casual, and unstructured community. More recent immigrants into the Lake Chapala region commented that though "traditional factors" such as climate and cost of living initially attracted them there, "eventually, their appreciation for the Mexican lifestyle and the unique nature of the foreign community had kept them in the area."

Truly hypothesized that of all of the immigrants in Lake Chapala, their primary motivations could be clustered into three distinct migration rationales: negative migration, positive migration, and importing a lifestyle. Truly used Everett Lee's[21] bimodal taxonomy of migrants to provide a definition for positively and negatively motivated migrants. Lee defined negative migrants as those who leave their home countries because they are dissatisfied with or persecuted, and positive migrants as people who leave their home countries because they wish to be part of a foreign community they appreciate and respect – without negative feelings toward their home countries. Truly argued that there was a third cluster of migrants who were "importing a lifestyle" into the Lake Chapala region. This third group had no negative feelings toward their home countries and had no positive regard for the local culture. Rather, they wanted to take advantage of the financial advantages a new country had to offer,

---

[20] Truly, D. (2002). International retirement migration and tourism along the Lake Chapala Riviera: developing a matrix of retirement migration behavior. *Tourism Geographies* 4(3), 261–281.

[21] Lee, E. (1966). A Theory of Migration. *Demography, 3,* 47-57.

while ignoring its culture and insulating themselves with others with similar migration motivations.

Facts and Figures about Retirement in Mexico

I have a confession to make. I don't know how many U.S. Baby Boomers live in Mexico. This is pretty disturbing considering I am the expert. But, like a number of data points in this book, finding precise numbers is a fluctuating and imperfect science.[22]

It is at least 30,000, but less than 65 million, and I suspect it's somewhere between 32,500 and 150,000 (Baby Boomers – not total expats), and I'm prepared to explain how I came to this conclusion (no matter how convoluted it may appear).

The State Department reports that there are about 1 million Americans living in Mexico.[23] The 2010 Mexican Census reported that number closer to 740,000.[24] This ~25% discrepancy could easily be explained by snowbirds – those who come to Mexico just for the winter, but don't live in the country year-round. But whether the figure is 740,000 or 1 million, even the lowest number is still double what it was 10 years ago.

I am going to work under the assumption that in 2016, there were 750,000 U.S. expats living full-time in Mexico. But not all of them are Baby Boomers. Let's pretend that they scaled perfectly and represented the same proportion of the population that Baby Boomers do in the United States (about 20%). If we did that, we would get a number as high as 150,000 Mexican Boomers. However, there are a couple of problems with this conclusion. First, it seems that more of the U.S. residents living in Mexico would be of

---

[22] Masterson, B. How many Americans live in Mexico? *The People's Guide to Mexico.*

[23] Bureau of Western Hemisphere Affairs. (2019, December 12). U.S. relations with Mexico: Bilateral relations fact sheet. *U.S. Department of State.*

[24] Censo de Población y Vivienda 2010.

retirement age, rather than equally scaled. Second, not every U.S. Baby Boomer has an equal likelihood of retiring in Mexico.

When I explore the demographic data that I collected for this book, only 1 to 5% percent of U.S. Baby Boomers are even likely candidates to move to Mexico (by likely candidates I mean that they share similar motivations, backgrounds, and economics as existing Mexico Boomers). If we assume that maybe 3.25 million Baby Boomers (at the high-end) are likely candidates to retire in Mexico, and we divide this number by the lowest end of that scale (1%) who actually do move to Mexico, we get 32,500 possible Baby Boomer retirees living south of the border.

If you want to get somewhere closer to the middle, consider this: In 2014, the Treasury Department made over 614,000 Social Security payments to residents living abroad (up from 242,000 just 10 years earlier). Again, if we simply scale these payments across the two populations, assuming that since 1/8 of the U.S. residents living abroad live in Mexico, they should get 1/8 of the Treasury checks. Using that methodology, we can estimate that about 77,000 Social Security payments are being sent to Mexico every month. However, that number is also probably quite low. In March of 2013, the Treasury Department began to require that all Social Security payments be made electronically, through direct deposit. What this change means is that most retirees can continue to collect their retirement benefits through their U.S.-based banks while using commonly accepted debit cards to make purchases abroad. The ease of receiving these payments makes it unlikely that most retirees living in Mexico would need to arrange for international payments from Social Security. So, it's likely that the Treasury's reporting of people receiving payments abroad significantly underestimates how many people are actually living outside the United States. Further adding to my suspicion that this number is far lower than reality, is a statement from a U.S. Embassy official in Mexico.[25] The official estimated that for every U.S. citizen who reports living in Mexico, there are 4 to 5 more who do not (as the law does not require U.S. citizens to do so).

So, there you have it. That is some of the data I relied on to come to my conclusion that between 32,500 and 150,000 U.S. Baby Boomers live full-time in Mexico. I suspect the number is even higher. I would not be surprised to learn that 250,000 U.S. Baby Boomers are living there right now. The speed in which Americans are arriving in Mexico has quickened. The result is that the gap between the reported data and the reality gets bigger and bigger every day. That is why determining a precise number remains such a challenge.

Television, Websites, Books and More

Whatever the actual number, the evidence I have presented so far should make it obvious that, over the last 10 years, the population of expats living in Mexico has been quickly growing.

It was Oscar Wilde (a Parisian expat himself) who opined, "Life imitates Art far more than Art imitates Life."[26] In the case of media related to the topic of exodus to Mexico, he may have a point. I don't have any doubt that the recent uptick in foreign lifestyle travel television programming and escape-based websites aimed at those interested in making a move south have certainly accelerated over the last decade. In fact, of the Baby Boomer expats I interviewed in Mexico, the majority of them moved after subscribing to international relocation websites and user groups. It was not unusual, and even common, to find recent retirees who arrived not knowing anyone in the city they were moving to. This is in sharp contrast to

---

[25] Masterson. Ibid.

[26] Life imitating art. (2019, November 19). *In Wikipedia.*

those who have settled in Mexico prior to the last 10 years. Those who have lived in Mexico a decade or longer are far more likely to have made the move after a recommendation from a friend or relative who successfully migrated to the area. For these Leading Edge Boomers, the likelihood that they would have moved to Mexico completely on their own was far less likely than the Trailing Edge, who have been arriving independently, and in larger and larger numbers.

In conjunction with that increased growth has come the creation of many for- and non-profit organizations, websites, blogs, podcasts, and television programs aimed at educating and selling to people interested in expatriation. Originally on the fringe of mainstream media, many of these organizations and programs are reporting significant increases in demand for their services and content. Over the last six years, one of the most popular expat websites, InternationalLiving.com, has had a two-and-a-half-fold increase in subscriptions to their magazine, International Living. They have also seen a three-fold increase in the number of people who attend conferences they conduct, educating people about retirement abroad.

More traditional organizations, such as AARP, have begun to devote more time and print space to the issue of international retirement as well. Through their website, AARP has been providing an ever increasing number of online resources for people who have, or plan to, retire in Mexico.[27]

Traditional financial planners like Merrill Lynch are also starting to include content on their websites about retirement in Mexico. What was once a luxury for those with excess capital has quickly become a financial strategy for those without.

---

[27] Golson, B. (2010 October). First-class urban amenities and charming palm-fringed villages draw retirees to the Puerto Vallarta region. *AARP.*

Investopedia.com provides a matrix on their site demonstrating that a married couple that receives the average monthly Social Security benefit payout ($1294.00 per person) could comfortably live in Mexico without any additional retirement funding.

Television offerings also point to an increase in the number of men and women interested in retiring outside of the United States. For example, the RLTV network is committed exclusively to programming for people over 50. The network's stars include Jane Pauley and Stanley Siegel, who host an international travel show titled "Stanley on the Go." A search of RLTV's content quickly uncovers Top Spot lists for retirement abroad, most of which include destinations in Mexico. There are other recurring features on the network that cater to individuals considering retirement abroad.

HGTV produces one of the most popular shows on living in Mexico, Mexico Life. In the show, local realtors help U.S. residents find their Mexican dream home. A review of the show reveals that compared to the U.S., housing prices are much lower in Mexico, and the homes are larger and contain upscale features, including beach views, lush gardens, and private pools.

Amazon also provides some clues about growing interest in Mexican retirement. A search for "retire in Mexico" revealed over 80 book titles, most of which were released in just the last few years. It is also interesting to point out that these titles seem to be a mix of professional and self-published books. It would appear that people who have moved to the region have become advocates for others to join them or that there is some significant interest and profit motive in publishing material on the subject. As a telling aside, a simultaneous search for "retire in Europe" only returns 15 books, far less than I would have expected for the perceived "safer" destinations in the world. A search for "retire in Florida" only returned 22 titles.

Just behind Google, YouTube is the second largest search engine on the internet and provides both amateur and professional video productions.[28] A search of "retire in Mexico" generated 124,000 related videos. A search of "retire in Europe" only generated 40,800 related videos. Again, as with Amazon, it appears that contemporary media production related to retirement in Mexico far exceeds other international retirement destinations, and if you're looking for both expert and native advice, there's no lack of it online.

The right of U.S. citizens to travel freely throughout the world is as old as the country itself. With few exceptions, Americans have enjoyed unparalleled access to almost every place in the world. In recent years, at least for Baby Boomers, international interests have focused on a destination much closer to home: Mexico. The reasons for this vary from its close proximity to the United States to its affordable cost of living. For older retirees, their chances for successful migration are largely dependent on welcoming and helpful communities in their destination countries. There are plenty of such communities in Mexico – from Lake Chapala to San Miguel de Allende, pockets of U.S. expats are eager to assist others in the transition to Mexican living. In addition to these established communities, an increase in internet usage among Baby Boomers has made exploring Mexican retirement easier and faster than ever before. Additionally, the regular appearance of Mexico-related television programming has made our southern neighbor more familiar and accessible. This accessibility has not only created an increase in interest in Mexican retirement, but it has motivated more people than ever to make the move.

---

[28] Mushroom Networks. How SD-WAN/Multi-WAN technology handles the data avalanche from YouTube.

CHAPTER 6

Motivations to Leave the United States
Methodology, Survey & Sampling
Profile & Demographic Findings

During my exploratory studies of Baby Boomer expatriation to Mexico, I formed three distinct hypotheses. First, Baby Boomers move to Mexico primarily due to their financial concerns in the United States. Second, Baby Boomers move to Mexico to escape ageism and the limiting stereotypes they perceive in the United States. Finally, that Baby Boomers move to Mexico in search of authentic communities they no longer believe exist in the United States.

These hypotheses came to me in a number of ways. First, the economic survey of Baby Boomers revealed that they were more likely than not to have an underfunded retirement. It seemed only natural to find out if that was the primary driver of expatriation into Mexico.

Second, as a sociology graduate student, the topics that interested me most were gerontology and community, (though not in any connected way, as they have become in this book). With regard to gerontology, I became particularly interested in assisted living centers and planned retirement communities. As part of my day job, I was often called to record people who were moved into these places as part of their recovery from a fall or other injury. I often wondered who benefited more from the orderly schedule of events, meals, hallways, and shared living spaces – the residents or the people paid to care for them? While the one-size-fits-all facility seemed to make a lot of sense for children finding their parents a home, it didn't light any fires in the hearts of those I interviewed, who generally felt pushed into living there and longed to return home. From this personal experience, I wondered how much a sense of good community benefited from impeccable order? To that end, I was inspired to read Jane Jacobs, who argued that some of our best communities sprout from places that are messy and spontaneous. As I pursued these Mexico Boomers, I wanted to find out if they thought the same thing.

With continued interest in community, I discovered authors like Wendell Berry[1] and Robert Putnam.[2] Both warned that community is in decline. While they have differing opinions as to why (i.e., technology, polarized politics, corporate influence, changes in lifestyle) both agree that there will be severe consequences for deteriorating civic engagement. I wanted to know if the Mexico Boomers perceived a deterioration as well, and how much did their need to be connected to an authentic community motivate them to seek out villages in Mexico?

Finally, my own curiosity, inspired by my personal desire to live somewhere else, motivated me to seek out books from people who had studied the subject and made a successful move. I discovered books like Leaving America: The New Expatriate Generation,[3] which details motivations for younger folks choosing to leave the U.S., Nomad Capitalist,[4] that dives into business considerations, and Third Culture Kids,[5] which assures parents that

---

[1] Berry, W. (1992). *Sex, Economy, & Community*. Pantheon Books.

[2] Putnam, R.D. (2000). *Bowling Alone: The Collapse and Revival of American Community* Touchstone: New York.

[3] Wennersten, 2008. Ibid.

[4] Henderson, 2018

5 Pollock & Van Reken, 1999

their children could not only survive, but thrive, living abroad. Within these hypotheses and reasoning, you will see a few classical sociological theorists, such as Durkheim,[6] Tonnies, and Cooley.

Brief Methodology

My first trip to Mexico was in August of 2009, to the Lake Chapala region just south of Guadalajara. There, I met with Dr. David Truly, at the time a Professor of Geography at Central Connecticut State University. Dr. Truly introduced me to the Lake Chapala Society (LCS), a local expat community dedicated to helping others successfully move to Mexico. During my visit to the LCS, I conducted many personal interviews with the organization's membership. In 2010, I submitted an online survey to the LCS, and I received hundreds of responses.

Since my 2010 study with the LCS, I have made six additional trips to Mexico. I have traveled to both coastal and inland villages. I have personally interviewed dozens of Baby Boomer expats and kept notes of our exchanges.

Over the last two years, I have been aggressively conducting online surveys with expat Baby Boomers all over Mexico, in towns like Puerto Morelos, Playa del Carmen, Merida, San Miguel de Allende, Cancun, Tulum, and more. In that time, I have collected hundreds of additional survey responses to help understand just who these Mexico Boomers are and why they left the United States.

Thanks to the internet, online forums, and social networks, I have also been able to have many virtual conversations while back home in Denver. I've been able to chat with other experts and researchers who have studied these subjects. I've even been able to

---

[6] Durkheim, E. (1893, 1984). *The Division of Labor in Society*. Translated by W.D. Halls. Macmillan. London, U.K.

submit sections of this book to trusted Mexico Boomers, who have corrected me on geographic and government issues and cultural misunderstandings.

I have combined all of this data with my own travel experiences and the input of experts to report the following findings and conclusions. I hope what I've collected over the last eight years provides you some valuable insight into U.S. Baby Boomers and what has motivated them to migrate to Mexico.

Survey Instrument and Sampling

The online survey I created was divided into four distinct sections, with questions related to; 1.) Demographic Information, 2.) Financial Information, 3.) Ageism and Alienation, and 4.) Community and Civic Engagement. It had a total of 76 questions. Survey questions were both multiple choice and measured on scales from Strongly Agree to Strongly Disagree. A few questions allowed for additional open-ended responses. The following findings and conclusions rely on about 500 responses, limited to retired U.S.-born Baby Boomers.

Findings: Demographic Profile

The first goal of this study was to create a demographic profile of the Mexico Boomers. The demographic variables I asked about were age, income, education, race, marital status, and political orientation. The purpose of this demographic survey was to identify if there was a certain type of person who is most likely to retire in Mexico. Conversely, we may also discover that there are many types of people who retire in Mexico and assuming a typical profile is an erroneous task.

Age

The average age of the Mexico Boomers is 59.6 years old. Based on age, a majority of the Mexico Boomers have retired younger than their retired counterparts in the United States. As of 2017, the average retirement age for men in the U.S. crept up to 65, and it was 62 for women.[7] Based on an average age of 59.6 for Mexico Boomers, it seems these retirees have found a way to get 3 to 5 more years out of their retirement.

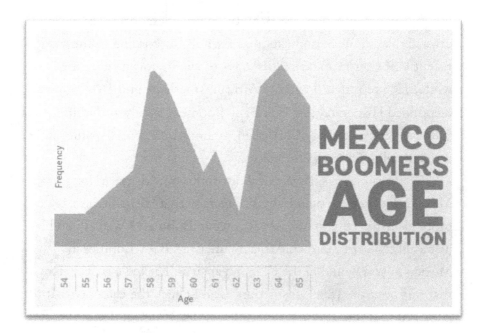

Let's also consider how long our respondents have already lived in Mexico. The median length of years lived in Mexico is 5, meaning that half of the respondents have lived in Mexico for less than five years and half have lived in Mexico for longer. Interestingly, the average time the Mexico Boomers have reported living in Mexico

---

[7] Munnell, H. (2017, October 15). Why the average retirement age is rising. *MarketWatch*.

is about 7.5 years. When compared to the median, what this tells us is that there is a significant group of people who have lived in Mexico for a pretty long time, while there is an even larger number of people who have just arrived over the last five years. Whether newly arrived, or already established, the data still suggest that people who retire in Mexico are, on average, doing it up to five years earlier than their U.S. counterparts.

Race

As noted earlier, the Baby Boomer generation is less racially diverse than the U.S. population as a whole. According to the most recent U.S. Census data, in 2010 64% of all Americans identified as white, 13% reported they were African American, and 16% percent responded Hispanic.[8] For U.S. Baby Boomers, race was distributed as follows: 72% white, 11.6% African American, 10.5% Hispanic, and the remaining 5.9% as other races.

I was curious if this racial distribution held true among Mexico Boomers. Would Baby Boomers with a Hispanic heritage be more likely to retire in Mexico than white Boomers? Would you be just as likely to run into an African-American Baby Boomer in Mexico as you would in the U.S.? To answer, I asked a survey item that mirrored the U.S. Census Bureau and check the category that indicated their race.

The survey results show that not only are the Mexico Boomers less racially diverse than the U.S. as a whole, they are far less racially diverse than their U.S. Boomer counterparts. Whereas 72% of U.S. Baby Boomers are white, 90% of the Mexico Boomers are white, meaning you would be far more likely to run into a white Baby Boomer in Mexico than in the United States.

---

[8] United State Census Bureau. (2011, March 24). 2010 Census shows America's diversity.

With regard to Hispanic Mexico Boomers, only 8.5% identified as such, showing that Hispanics are no more likely to choose retirement in Mexico over their U.S. counterparts, and being Hispanic might actually make one less likely to consider a Mexican retirement.

Most surprising was that only 0.3% of survey participants reported being African American. Because African Americans make up nearly 12% of the Baby Boomer generation, it's worth diving into this finding and considering some possible explanations.

African Americans of the Baby Boomer generation have had far tougher financial struggles than their white counterparts. They have had historically low wages compared to whites.[9] Fewer have broken into the middle class.[10] Even into 2016, median household income for whites was $56,041 as compared to $39,490 for African Americans, and they make up 22% of all people in the U.S. who live in poverty, including 34% of all African-American children.[11] All-in-all, a black person in the United States is more than twice as likely to live in poverty as their white counterparts.[12]

With regard to retirement savings, instead of improving over time, the gap between black and white family savings has actually widened. As of 2013, the average white family had $130,000 in retirement savings compared to $19,000 for African Americans. With regard to general wealth, between 1963 and 2013,[13] whites have accumulated over four times more in assets than their African-American counterparts. While we would like to believe that the U.S.

---

[9] Minority News. (2019, December 13). Black Baby Boomers eye uncertain retirement.

[10] Statista Research Department. (2015, December 9). Percentage of U.S. adult population belonging to the middle class from 1971 to 2015, by race and ethnicity.

[11] Kids Count Data Center. (2019). Children in poverty by race and ethnicity in the United States. *The Annie E. Casey Foundation.*

[12] Kaiser Family Foundation. (2018). Poverty rate by race/ethnicity.

[13] Brooks, R. (2017, March 9). The retirement crisis facing African Americans. *Forbes.*

has been moving toward more racial parity, the facts are that it has been drifting apart.[14]

Working within the primary hypothesis that people who move to Mexico do so because they can't afford to retire in the United States, we would expect to see African-Americans overrepresented when compared to the racial distribution in the United States. But we actually find the opposite – those in the U.S. with the most dire financial retirement situation (African Americans) are the least likely to retire in Mexico.

What we may conclude is that a Mexican retirement is actually a luxury most afforded to whites, who have the historical income, savings, retirement funds, and existing communities needed to make a comfortable Mexican retirement transition.

Having money during migration matters because it allows for a safety net should a migrant face any challenge, make a mistake, or simply suffer bad luck during the course of a move. For a majority of African-American retirees, that cushion does not exist, meaning that an unsuccessful migration could be catastrophic, or simply not possible in the first place.

The criticism some African Americans endured for not leaving New Orleans before and during Hurricane Katrina helps highlight this unique predicament.[15] This criticism came from uninformed outsiders who had a hard time imagining how someone could have zero resources needed to pick up and move at a moment's notice. But keep in mind that, as the storm arrived, the government was not offering any travel vouchers or housing assistance outside the city. African Americans without savings,

---

[14] Patten, E. (2016, July 1). Racial, gender wage gaps persis in U.S. despite some progress. Pew Research Center.

[15] CBS News. (2005, September 5). Race an issue in Katrina response.

transportation, or family up north had nowhere to go, and even if they did, they had no way to get there.

In a broader sense, the same is true for African-American retirees. No matter how financially beneficial a Mexican retirement may be for them, it's logistically unattainable. And for those who may be able to afford a move, their migration may be further hindered by the fact that African Americans have fewer friends, family, peers, or established migration networks in Mexico compared to their white counterparts.

As noted earlier in the book, migrants who move to a new country where they have existing family, or an existing racial or ethnic base are far more likely to have a successful migration than those who do not. With regard to African Americans, there is little in the way of a rich and stable migrant community to ease the burdens of late-life migration and welcome them to their new home. This is not to say that African Americans who do move to Mexico are not accepted or assisted by their established white peers (they are), but they do arrive at a financial, cultural and familial disadvantage that can severely hamper their chances for continued success.

Taking all of the above into consideration, it makes sense that African Americans would be underrepresented compared to the rest of the Mexico Boomer population. If the existing Mexico Boomers have an interest in creating a more racially diverse Mexican retirement population, they will have to consider creative ways to reach non-whites back in the U.S. and assure them that the expat community in Mexico has safety nets to make a successful move down south.

Education
I also asked participants about their level of education, ranging from some high school through doctoral and professional degrees. I then compared these answers against Educational

Attainment by Generation data gathered by the U.S. Census Bureau.[16]

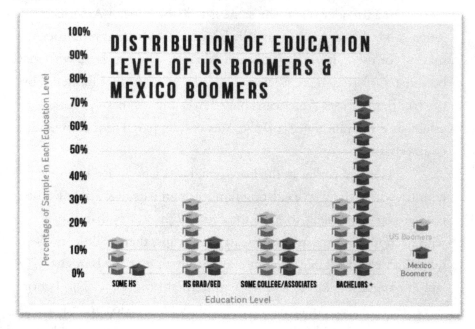

The graphic above shows that, compared to their U.S. counterparts, the Mexico Boomers are far more educated than the general population. In fact, if the Mexico Boomers were their own generation, they would be the most educated generation in history, even more educated than Gen Xers and Millennials.[17]

U.S. Baby Boomer Education Levels
- High School Diploma/GED - 31%
- Some College/Associates - 27%
- Bachelor's Degree - 19%
- Masters Degree - 9%
- Professional/Doctoral Degree - 3.6%

[16] Russell, C. (2015). *The Baby Boom*. New Strategist Press.
[17] Russell, 2015. Ibid.

Mexico Boomers Education Levels

- High School Diploma/GED - 12%
- Some College/Associates - 14%
- Bachelor's Degree - 36%
- Masters Degree - 25%
- Professional/Doctoral Degree - 13%

Mexico Boomers have almost double the number of Bachelor's Degrees, almost triple the number of Master's Degrees, and over three times the number of Professional and Doctoral degrees as Baby Boomers living in the U.S.

Because higher degrees of education usually translate into higher salaries, this factor can help explain Mexico Boomer's large number of upper-income residents. Higher levels of education can also translate into higher levels of social liberalism. According to Neil Gross, a sociology professor at Colby College, "There's some pretty good evidence that going to college leads people to have more liberal attitudes on social issues, in particular on issues of tolerance, of difference and issues of gender equity." Indeed, we also find that the Mexico Boomers are more likely to describe themselves as liberal compared to their U.S. counterparts, something we will continue to dissect below.

Political Orientation

To measure political orientation, I asked survey participants two questions. First, I asked them to identify themselves on a scale ranging from very conservative to very liberal. Here's how Baby Boomers in the U.S. describe their political leanings (2014): 21%

liberal, 33% moderate, and 44% report conservative.[18] Here's how the Mexico Boomers from our survey describe their political leanings: 56% liberal, 20% moderate, and 17% conservative (the remaining 7% said they didn't know which way they leaned).

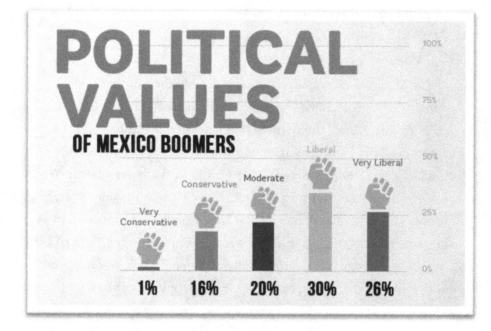

We can see that the Mexico Boomers are more than two-and-a-half times more likely to report being liberal than their U.S. counterparts and half as likely to identify as conservative. These findings corroborate my earlier inclination that a more educated population will be more socially liberal. That certainly seems to be the case with the Mexico Boomers, though not exclusively, as nearly 1 in 5 Mexico Boomers still reports a socially conservative worldview.

Second, I asked whether respondents identified as Democrat, Republican, other/independent, or don't know.

---

[18] Jones, J.M. (2015, January 29). U.S. Baby Boomers more likely to identify as conservative. *Gallup.*

Here's how party lines break across all ages in the United States (2017): 31% Democrat, 24% Republican, and 42% report other/independent.[19] Among Baby Boomers in the U.S. (2018), it looks like this: 37% Democrat, 34% Republican, and 29% other/independent.[20] Baby Boomers are more likely to report Republican than the rest of the population. They are also more likely to identify with a political party than identify as independent. This is contrary to the general U.S. population, which is more likely to identify as independent than with a specific political party.

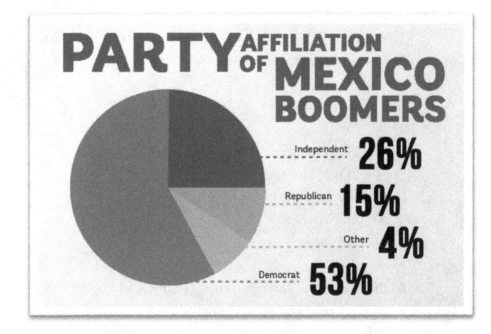

With regard to the Mexico Boomers: 53% are Democrat, 15% are Republican, 26% are Independent, and 4% report as "Other." The Mexico Boomers and U.S. Boomers identify as

[19] Political party strength in the United States. (2019, December 9). In *Wikipedia.*
[20] Miles, K. (2018, November 6). Political party affiliation for Millennials versus Baby Boomers. *Branded Polls.*

independent at about the same rate. However, the distance between Democrats and Republicans is significant. The Mexico Boomers are more than three times as likely to identify as Democrat than Republican, as opposed to a close split back in the United States. It's also worth noting that, on average, a Democratic family has higher incomes than a Republican family.[21] So, going back to my previous discussion of income, it should not be any surprise that well-educated Democrats with higher than average incomes outnumber any other group within the Mexico Boomers.

Marital Status

According to our survey results, the marital status of all the Mexico Boomers breaks out as follows:

- 56% Married
- 25% Single
- 21% Divorced
- 11% Widowed
- 8% Remarried
- 4% Separated
- 1% Other

To the math whiz, these percentages do not add up to 100%. Keep in mind that some people reporting "single" may have also reported as "divorced" or "widowed," or some "married" respondents may have also indicated that they are "separated." Even though I've decided not to break those cross-relationships out, I still feel presenting all of the responses is a little more enlightening than limiting them to married, single, and divorced.

---

[21] Blankenship, A. (2017, October 18). Who is richer? Democrats or Republicans? The answer probably won't surprise you. *Budget and the Bees.*

Overall, 56% of the Mexico Boomers report being married. While at first glance that doesn't seem remarkable, there is something quite interesting when we break them out by gender.

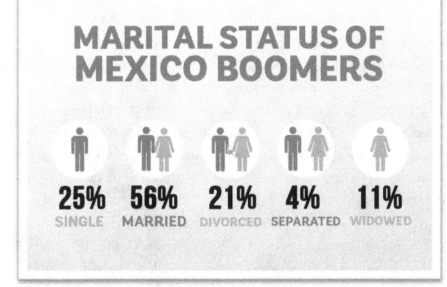

Consider the following: 61% of all survey respondents in this book were female. Only 39% identified as male (as a side note, I did allow for "transgendered" and "other" categories for the gender question but had zero responses for either).[22] I have concluded that, from my own personal experience and that of others I spoke to, women do indeed outnumber men.

---

[22] Some of the limits of online surveys like this one is that they do not reach everyone they claim to report on. For example, it must be said that the data in this book really only represent Baby Boomer expats in Mexico who have an internet connection and participate in online forums or communities. Based on these responses, we could conclude that there are more expat women than men in Mexico, or we could conclude that women are more likely than men to have an internet connection and participate in online forums or communities.

Even more interesting, the data show that women are almost twice as likely as men to arrive in Mexico either single or divorced. In fact, 39% percent of the female Mexico Boomers surveyed reported being either single, divorced, widowed, or separated as compared to only 22% of men.

One of the unexpected outcomes of this imbalance was the discovery of a vibrant Mexico Boomer dating scene. Anecdotally, I was told by some male Mexico Boomers that Mexican expat communities were a great place to meet single women. I was also told by a number of single women that a bit of infighting has occurred for their attention. The data do seem to suggest that Mexico Boomer women are more likely to be single than men, and that there are a lot more of them – lending some credence to the wink-wink single's scene I have been assured is alive and well within these expat communities.

In total, about 56% of the Mexico Boomers are married. This number is also low, compared to a 70% marriage rate for Boomers still back in the States (including remarriages). If we view these numbers through the money hypothesis, it makes sense that more women than men are retiring in Mexico – especially single women. In Chapter 2, I argued that single people, especially women, are far more likely to struggle financially in retirement than married couples with dual incomes and assets.[23] Mexico may provide single Baby Boomers of both genders one solution to money trouble and may be even more attractive to single women who have historically lower wages and suffer more severe financial consequences after a divorce. Also, in reviewing the data from my original Mexico Boomer survey in 2008, it appears this trend has remained steady, indicating that the

---

[23] Woodruff, M. (2013, February 8). There are way too many single Baby Boomers. *Business Insider.*

arrival of single female Baby Boomers in Mexico is not a recent development but one that has been consistent over time.

Archetype Demographic Conclusion

If we had to identify a typical Mexico Boomer based on this demographic survey data, that person would look something like this:

> A married 59-year-old college educated Caucasian with a higher than average income, who votes Democrat, is social liberally, and has lived in Mexico for just about 5 years.

We'll continue to build on this archetype as we explore the other motivations Mexico Boomers reported as to why they left the United States.

PART III.

THE MEXICO BOOMERS – WHY THEY LEAVE

CHAPTER 7

Why They Leave
Hypothesis 1: Money
Cost of Living, Healthcare, Meaningful Employment
& Early Retirement
Results & Discussion

Hypothesis 1: Money

By now it should be obvious that most Baby Boomers on the cusp of retirement are facing dire financial situations. Their retirement accounts were hit hard by the 2008 financial crisis. They have little equity in their homes. Few can count entirely on their pensions and retirement savings. Most are banking on Social Security to get them through. They have more debt than ever, and they are sandwiched between caring for their own parents and their adult children who are also facing economic troubles. Based on this information, the idea that Baby Boomers may move to Mexico in an attempt to save money (or stretch retirement dollars) seems like a natural and probable conclusion.

For anyone in the U.S. facing tough economic times, Mexico is attractive. Consider the following information:

- Consumer prices are over 64% higher in the United States than Mexico.
- Grocery prices are almost 70% higher in the United States than in Mexico.
- Restaurant prices are almost 90% higher in the United States than in Mexico.
- Rent prices are nearly 200% higher in the United States than in Mexico.

Health Care Costs in Mexico

For Baby Boomers considering retirement in Mexico, it's important to understand the local healthcare system, especially for an aging population where health problems may become more frequent. One striking benefit of the Mexican health care system is that retirees can expect to pay 50% less in Mexico for the same treatments, procedures, and prescriptions than those in the United States.[24] But these savings come with a few warnings and additional considerations.

Though many Baby Boomers harbor misconceptions about health care in Mexico,[25] the reality is that the health care system is considered quite good. Generally speaking, the medical facilities and health care providers in Mexico are on par with what is available in the United States. In Mexico's larger cities, including Mexico's top five expat communities, there are well-maintained and major medical centers. Many of the doctors practicing in Mexico receive the same

---

[24] Murray, D. (2019). Mexican healthcare is excellent and affordable. *International Living*.

[25] Murray, 2019. Ibid.

medical training as those in the U.S.– often at the same medical schools.

Over the last 15 years, this combination of excellent care and low costs have fostered a movement of "medical tourism," in which U.S. residents plan vacations around receiving medical care in Mexico.[26] These treatments include cancer care, dental care, and elective weight-loss surgeries. Medical tourism really underscores the quality, availability, and low costs of healthcare in Mexico and should provide some reassurance to expats looking for local care.

Mexico has a number of federally supported health care plans. The two most recognizable are Instituto Mexicano del Seguro Social (IMSS) and Seguro Popular. But not all expats are eligible for IMSS and Seguro Popular. U.S. residents who live in Mexico and work for a Mexican company are automatically enrolled in the IMSS program, with a small portion of their wages deducted each month to help pay for their health care. Those not employed by a Mexican company but are legal permanent residents of Mexico, may be eligible for benefits through Seguro Popular. The cost of Seguro Popular for non-citizens is on a sliding scale and is primarily dependent upon your income.

Those who do have a medical emergency and do not have insurance through either of Mexico's federal health insurance programs should assume they will pay for care out-of-pocket at the time of treatment. Fortunately, because so many Americans take advantage of healthcare in Mexico, most providers have all the paperwork needed to be reimbursed by existing insurance companies. However, not all U.S.-based health insurance companies cover all overseas health issues. If you plan on traveling abroad, it's important to call your insurance provider ahead of time to verify your coverage.

---

[26] Dickson, C. (2017, March 22). A boom in medical tourism to Mexico predicted in Obamacare ends. *Yahoo News*.

If coverage is not available, there are short-term travel insurance programs available from many companies. While unusual, there have been cases in which U.S. citizens have been detained until they have been able to satisfy their hospital bills.[27] Remember, even though health care can be a heck of a lot cheaper in Mexico, catastrophic injuries or illness can still generate catastrophic bills.

For Baby Boomers whose sole source of health insurance is Medicare, I've got somber news: Except in very rare cases, expats cannot use Medicare to pay for treatments outside the United States.[28] Because of this, it's not uncommon for Baby Boomer expats in Mexico to revisit the United States every 90 days for non-emergency medical treatments and to restock prescriptions. But for some of the folks I interviewed (especially those with chronic conditions), the lack of Medicare in Mexico made a move down south impossible. This realization highlights the fact that for some Baby Boomers, Medicare and health care create invisible borders for those who might prefer to retire somewhere else.

Results

To answer questions about money, I first wanted to know how many of the Mexico Boomers were truly money motivated. When asked if economic factors were the biggest motivator in their decision to move to Mexico, the group was pretty evenly split – for about half the respondents, money was the biggest reason they hit the road.

Knowing that respondents had lived an average of 7.5 years in Mexico, I then asked for how many of them was money still the most important reason they live in Mexico. Thirty-seven percent said

---

[27] Rudavsky, S. (2017, July 21). Premature baby held in Mexican hospital until bill was paid arrives in U.S. *USA TODAY.*

[28] Mexperience. (2019, October 14). Is U.S. Medicare available in Mexico?

it was. But when asked if money was no longer a factor in where you lived, would you move back to the United States, only 8% said yes. This finding is significant because it tells us that even though money remains front-and-center in about a third of the Mexico Boomers' minds, it isn't a strong enough variable to make them leave Mexico. For a majority of the Mexico Boomers, there's something else besides money that's keeping them there.

For some historical perspective, I asked participants to think back to 20 years ago and identify where they thought their retirement funding was going to come from. The top five answers were:

1.) Social Security – 20%
2.) 401k - 20%
3.) Pension – 19%
4.) Personal Savings - 14%
5.) Sale of a Home – 12.5%

Then I asked participants to indicate where their retirement funding was *actually* coming from. The top five answers were:

1.) Social Security – 30%
2.) Pension – 22%
3.) Sale of a Home – 14%
4.) Personal Savings - 13%
5.) Personal Investments – 12%

There are two notable findings here. First is that the 401k was imagined to be the second most significant source for retirement funding. The reality is that it didn't even make the top five. This would lend credence to the possibility that at least some (if not a majority) of the Mexico Boomers suffered brutal stock market consequences after the 2008 financial crisis.

Second, reliance on Social Security to fund retirement took about a 10% bump compared to expectations. More of the Mexico Boomers rely on Social Security as their primary retirement funding than had planned to. Perhaps that is an outcome of youthful optimism, or perhaps it is further evidence that a significant group of the Mexico Boomers either poorly planned or ran into a financial anomaly over the last two decades.

With regard to poor planning, another interesting finding is that one-third of respondents admitted that 20 years ago, they didn't even have a retirement plan! So, I wanted to know how retirement planning affected one's likelihood to retire in Mexico. I asked how solid they perceived their current retirement funding. Forty-five percent reported that their retirement funding is in line with where they thought it would be. Thirty-two percent reported that retirement funding was a real concern. Twenty-three percent reported they actually had more money for retirement than planned. Based on this information, it would appear that about 1 in 3 Mexico Boomers have less money than they thought they would, while the rest are either at or above their 20-year expectations.

Now that we know Boomers' sources of retirement income, and how they compare to expectations, let's take a look at how much money is actually making it to Mexico.

Retirement Income

To measure current retirement income, I asked participants to indicate their annual household income ranging from $20,000 to more than $100,000, using the same increments as existing U.S. Census data on the income of retired people. I compared the reported income of U.S. residents 65 and older to the retirement income reported by the Mexico Boomers. I then ran a statistical analysis to determine if there was a notable income difference between the Mexico Boomers and U.S. retirees.

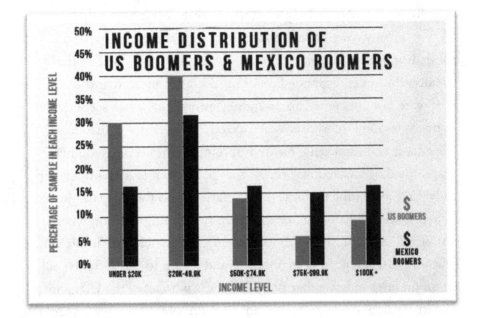

This comparison shows that the Mexico Boomers are not any worse off financially than their U.S. counterparts. Looking at the image above, we can see that the income distribution for Mexico Boomers in the middle class is about the same as those in the U.S. However, you are twice as likely to run into low-income retired individuals in the U.S. as you are in Mexico. And at the top income levels, a retired Mexico Boomer is twice as likely to be a high-income earner than a retired person in the United States.

These results are important because they show that even though half of survey respondents said money was their primary motivator for leaving the U.S., they were not any worse off financially than retirees who stayed behind (in every case, they're better). What is more likely is that someone who worries about their money is more likely to consider Mexico than someone who simply has less. It also appears that being well off, in combination with some other variable or variables, is a better predictor of one's likelihood of migrating to Mexico than low income. Further into the chapter we'll look at those additional variables and explore the possible connections.

Finally, when asked plainly if money was the biggest motivator in their decision to move to Mexico, about half of the Mexico Boomers responded yes. This does not mean that the other half were not concerned about money, just that it was a secondary concern to something else. When asked "Now that you live in Mexico, is economics the most important factor keeping you here?" respondents answered that economics plays even less of a role, with only 36% indicating that it is the primary reason they stay in Mexico. When asked "if economic factors were not an influence on where you lived" 86% of Mexico Boomers said they would stay in Mexico, with only 10% reporting that they would return to the U.S. Overall, these findings indicate that Baby Boomers who leave the U.S. and live in Mexico would prefer to remain there even if money was no longer a problem.

Meaningful Employment and Early Retirement

For those of us not part of the 1%, most of our income is derived from employment. If our prospects for employment wither, so too may our motivations to stay put. That is why it's important to explore employment opportunities as we continue to explore the financial motivations of the Mexico Boomers.

U.S. Baby Boomers create a true paradox for social scientists and employers. On one hand, economists warn that the mass exodus of Baby Boomer retirees could create a shortage of skilled workers.[29] On the other hand, Baby Boomer workers have been called "a potential drag on corporate performance and financial resources."[30] For those who believe the latter, there may be motivation to avoid hiring Baby Boomers in the first place, rather than implementing training or resource programs to address perceived professional gaps.

Further disadvantaging Baby Boomer employees is the fact that health insurance for those over 55 can be more than double the cost of employees under 45.[31] That may be an unbearable cost for small companies and a difficult one for large, as health care costs in the U.S. continue to soar.[32]

If there is any question as to whether these circumstances are creating fewer opportunities for meaningful employment among Baby Boomers in the United States, let's take a look at a few ominous facts:

- In 2016, there were nearly 21,000 age discrimination complaints filed with the Equal Employment Opportunity Commission.[33]
- A younger worker is 40 percent more likely to be offered an interview than an older worker.[34]

---

[29] Bjelland, M.J., Bruyere, S.M., von Schrader, S., Houtenville, A.J., Ruiz-Quintanilla, A. & Webber, D.A. (2010). Age and disability employment discrimination: Occupational rehabilitation implications. *Journal of Occupational Rehabilitation, 20*(4), 456-471.

[30] Callanan, G.A. & Greenhaus, J.H. (2008). The Baby Boom generation and career management: A call to action. *Advances in Developing Human Resources, 10*(1), 70-85.

[31] Penner, R.G., Perun, P. & Steuerle, C.E. (2002). Legal and institutional impediments to partial retirement and part-time work by older workers. *Urban Institute.*

[32] Conover, C. (2012, December 22). The cost of health care: 1958 vs. 2012. *Forbes.*

[33] Terrell, K. (2017, November 7). Age discrimination goes online. *AARP Bulletin.*

[34] Lahey, J.N. (2008). Age, women and hiring: An experimental study. *Journal of Human Resources, 43*(1), 30-56.

- Older workers are perceived as less likely to accept supervision from younger managers.[35]
- Younger employees may see Baby Boomer coworkers as competition and barriers to professional advancement.[36]

While these facts highlight the barriers Baby Boomers face to new employment, let's take a look at the dangers for those currently employed:

- 16% of current Baby Boomer retirees report being forced out by an employer or given an early retirement incentive.[37]
- In 2015, 45% of job hunters over the age of 55 had been unemployed for nearly 7 months.[38]
- Baby Boomers who do find second careers suffer a 20%-39% wage loss as compared to their previous jobs.

These frustrations have caused some Baby Boomers to stop looking for work all together. In fact, layoffs after the 2008 financial crisis drove at least 1.4 million U.S. Baby Boomers to collect early Social Security after they were unable to find comparable employment.[39] In light of these facts, it seems fair to ask Mexico Boomers how opportunities for meaningful employment motivated their moves to Mexico.

---

[35] DePillis, L. (2016, August 4). Baby Boomers are taking on ageism – and losing. *The Washington Post.*

[36] Kittling, N.M & Wolf, F.Z. Implications of an ageing workforce. *Fisher & Phillips LLP, Chicago Office.*

[37] Cole, M. (2015, February, 3). The surprising reasons Baby Boomers retire. *The Fiscal Times.*

[38] Rafter, D. (2016, June 7). 5 ways to handle a forced early retirement. *Killer Aces Media.*

[39] Gordon, C. (2013, May 3). More than 1 million Baby Boomers are secretly unemployed. *AOL News.*

My data show that the Mexico Boomers retire five years earlier than their U.S. counterparts. Throughout my interviews, many individuals cited a lack of substantial employment as a big reason for that. When asked, 92% either agreed or strongly agreed that age discrimination made it hard for them to find meaningful work in the U.S. Only eight percent had never felt discriminated against. Additionally, as for a general feeling of respect, 76% of respondents feel like U.S. citizens no longer respect their elders.

The double-edged sword of all this is that, for almost all Mexico Boomers, working in Mexico is impossible. Even if they wanted to pursue meaningful employment, they would be locked out due to residency or tax and benefit restrictions. This may explain why philanthropy and community service are so high among the Mexico Boomers, something we'll explore in the coming chapters.

CHAPTER 8

Why They Leave
Hypothesis 2: Ageism and Discrimination
Ageism, Discrimination, and Stereotypes, Respect for Elders
and Youth Culture

Ageism is "prejudice or discrimination against a particular
age-group and especially the elderly." Compared to other forms of
discrimination, such as sexism or racism, ageism still receives
"second-class treatment."[1] But for older adults who experience
ageism, the effects are significant, both physically and financially.
Physically, individuals who ignore ageism and maintain a positive
self-perception of ageing, live an average of 7.5 years longer than
those who do not.[2] Financially, there is substantial evidence that
recent anti-ageism employment laws have done little to protect older
workers, and this lack of employment protection compounds
financial troubles for the majority of Baby Boomers who have little-
to-no retirement savings.[3]

---

[1] Cohen, A. (2009, November 6). After 40 years, age discrimination still gets second-
class treatment. *The New York Times.*

[2] Levy, B.R., Slade, M.D., Kunkel, S.R. & Kasl, S.V. (2002). Longevity increased by
positive self-perceptions of aging. *Journal of Personality and Social Psychology, 83*(2),
261-270.

[3] Neumark, D. & Button, P. (2013). Did age discrimination protections help older
workers weather the Great Recession? *The National Bureau of Economic Research.*

Social psychologists believe that our earliest perceptions of one another are first formed by the recognition of three major characteristics: gender, race, and age. The reason we rely so heavily on these characteristics today may stem from thousands of years of psychological evolution in which humans needed to quickly understand who was in their tribe and who was not.[4] When we have very little information to go on, we tend to rely on the obvious. And, in most cases, there is no hiding your gender, race, or age.

Today, humans do not face the same kind of physical environmental threats that plagued younger tribal species. Thus, we may not need our brains to work as hard as they have in the past to make quick assumptions to protect us. But evolution can be slow and stubborn. For example, men no longer need beards to protect their faces from the elements, wisdom teeth are nothing but an archaic pain, and the tailbone is just a leftover from our time in the trees. Even our appendix no longer seems to serve any necessary purpose.[5] Within our own bodies, we can recognize that evolutionary biology is not always in lockstep with the realities of today's world – and, unfortunately, some mental processes are no different.

The reality is that our mental recognition of another's age creates a number of internal assumptions that guide how we might interact with that person. For example, we may make age-based assumptions about a person's political orientation, physical strength, cognitive ability, musical preferences, and values.[6] When a number of these assumptions are combined and continually passed around a society, or passed down through generations, a stereotype is born. A stereotype is "a widely held but fixed and oversimplified image or

---

[4] Schaller, M., Gideon Conway III, L. & Peavy, K.M. (2010). Evolutionary Processes. In *The Sage Handbook of Prejudice, Stereotyping and Discrimination*, pp. 81-96.

[5] Live Science. (2012, July 11). 5 Useless body parts.

[6] Nelson, T.D. (2005). *Ageism: Stereotyping and prejudice against older persons.* Massachusetts Institute of Technology Press.

idea of a particular type of person or thing." According to the American Psychological Association, Baby Boomers have been stereotyped as ambitious workaholics who are generally optimistic and who believe in teamwork and cooperation.[7] This is in contrast to their "Traditionalist" parents who were stereotyped as patient and practical people who respect authority, follow the rules, and believe in the value of a hard day's work.

When it comes to ageism, and the stereotypes associated with getting older, few of them are flattering or empowering. In Oregon, the state circulated material to caregivers of the elderly, which asked them to self-assess their own stereotypes. This was done in an attempt to improve care by making sure caregivers treated each elderly person as an individual rather than as a member of a stereotyped group. Through this process, Oregon asked caregivers to be aware of some of the commonly held myths about the elderly. These myths include that people become more similar age as they age; elderly people have no worries; elderly people have no interest in sexual activity; elderly people are slow to learn, less intelligent, and more forgetful; and that elderly people are inflexible and crabby. SeniorPlanet.org has also posted a list of popular myths about older adults, which include assumptions that older people have a hard time getting around by themselves; older people miss more work due to illness; older people are lonely and depressed; and that older people are obsessed with death and dying. While there is little evidence that any of this is true, these are the stereotypes that saddle most seniors.

Why do these stereotypes exist? What possible purpose could ageism serve? Richard Dyer argues that stereotypes act as "a way of substituting order for the great blooming, buzzing confusion of

---

[7] American Psychological Association. (2005). Generation Stereotypes. Vol. 36(6).

reality."[8] So, while we may stereotype older people as less eager to work, as tired, and as lazy, ironically, we do this because we are lazy ourselves; because these stereotypes help us simplify what is actually a very robust and dynamic portion of our population.

Historically, it is not hard to find records of marginalized people inspired to pack-up and move elsewhere due to discrimination (both perceived and real). Beginning in 1910, a "Great Migration" of African Americans moved out of the segregated U.S. South and headed to Northern cities in search of better social and economic opportunities. After the 1947 independence of India, minority Muslims headed north to form Pakistan. And after the Holocaust of WWII, Jews moved into present day Israel. Now, I certainly don't mean to put the frustrations of our aging population in the same category as those who survived the Holocaust. What I do mean to do is highlight how small groups of people have been willing to take on extraordinary challenges to create a space they can call their own. Some of today's Baby Boomers may feel no different.

Overall, my findings support the literature in that over 70% of Mexico Boomers see their generation as negatively stigmatized by the media. In fact, about ¾ of those interviewed believe the U.S. has lost its respect for elders. Here are some other related insights:

- About 75% do not believe news programming is aimed at them
- About 85% do not believe U.S. advertising is aimed at them
- About 92% do not believe most magazines are aimed at them

---

[8] Dyer, R. (1999). The role of stereotypes. *In Media Studies: A Reader, 2nd Edition.* Edinburgh University Press.

- About 92% believe there is too much emphasis on looking and acting young in the U.S.

In general, three out of four Mexico Boomers think that people have a poor opinion of them because of their age. Most believe they are ignored by, or excluded from, the media. They don't see a lot of material or programming they can relate to. And they don't see a lot of people who look like they do portrayed positively in society. Rather, they see a constant embrace of youth culture and youthful again, two things that are out of lockstep with their own priorities.

CHAPTER 9

Why They Leave
Hypothesis 3: Authentic Community
Results and Conclusions

In addition to financial and employment concerns, social scientists worry about Baby Boomers' emotional and mental health. Some researchers have concluded that Baby Boomers collectively are less optimistic than their preceding and succeeding generations. The Pew Research Center has described Boomers as the gloomiest of these three generations.[1] This sense of gloom seems persistent and has been documented for over two decades. Some argue that the dark cloud of gloom stems from the following concerns[2]:

- Financial Status
- Personal Accomplishments
- Lower Standard of Living
- Lack of Professional Progress
- Outside Factors Dictating Success

---

[1] Pew Research Center. (2008). Baby Boomers: The gloomiest generation.
[2] Pew Research Center, 2008. Ibid.

Younger Baby Boomers especially are more likely to share the current generation's belief that "success in life is determined mainly by outside forces."[3] This pessimistic orientation towards success may be informed by feeling that being part of a larger birth cohort means more competition for schools, jobs, and resources.[4] This, combined with money trouble, a lower standard of living, high stress, and few meaningful employment opportunities could be contributing to the rise in Baby Boomer depression and low quality of life scores.[5]

More and more research shows that depression and personal dissatisfaction could be alleviated through cognitive exercise and good community, including meaningful opportunities for volunteerism and civic engagement.[6] People who study senior cohousing identify mental exercise, civic engagement, group decision making, and meaningful opportunities to participate within the community as important dimensions for community satisfaction.[7] The White House Conference on Aging even ranked good community over affordability in its list of priorities related to retirement policy planning.[8]

Good community may also protect against cognitive decline.[9] The Centers for Disease Control believe that preventing cognitive

---

[3] Pew Research Center, 2008. Ibid.

[4] Yang, Y. (2008). Social inequalities in happiness in the United States, 1972 to 2004: An age-period-cohort analysis. *American Sociological Review, 73*(2), 204-226.

[5] Kapes, B.A. (2018, October 8). Depression and Baby Boomers: How having it all may be too much. *PsychCentral.*

[6] Simson, S. & Wilson, L. (2006). *Civic Engagement and the Baby Boomer Generation: Research, Policy, And Practice Perspectives.* Howorth Press: Binghamton, NY.

[7] Glass, Anne P. (2009). Aging in a Community of Mutual Support: The Emergence of an Elder Intentional Cohousing Community in the United States. *Journal of Housing for the Elderly.*

[8] White House Conference on Aging (2005). The Booming Dynamics of Aging: From Awareness to Action. *Executive Summary.*

[9] Hikichi, H., Kondo, K., Takeda, T. & Kawachi, I. (2017). Social interaction and cognitive decline: Results of a 7-year community intervention. *Alzheimers Dementia: Translational Research & Clinical Interventions, 3*(1), 23-32.

decline can extend the health of Baby Boomers.[10] Simson and Wilson also found a positive correlation between cognitive exercise and quality of life.[11]

While there seems to be consensus that meaningful community is important for healthy aging,[12] some researchers believe we should not be too quick to overlook the value of a strong sense of personal independence among our older population.[13] Breheny and Stephens argue that seniors perceive independence as a "marker of successful aging" and dependency on others as a fault. Though personal independence and community connectedness seem like potentially contradictory terms, social scientists reconcile the two by arguing that opportunities for reciprocity in individual exchanges can actually preserve a senior's sense of self-reliance, while at the same time improving social connectedness. Reciprocity (exchanges between community members that help each other to an equal extent) may provide an opportunity for community building, which does not leave either party feeling that they are in a dependent position.

While researchers believe good community holds a key to healthy aging, cultural critics fear those bonding opportunities are slipping away. As early as 1992, Wendall Berry warned that the media and consumerism were breeding distrust and that community was being "destroyed by the desires and ambitions of both private and public life."[14] Berry believed the future would hold a "conventional

---

[10] Centers for Disease Control and Prevention and The Merck Company Foundation. (2000). The state of aging and health in America.

[11] Simson & Wilson, 2006. Ibid.

[12] Koelen, M., Eriksson, M. & Cattan, M. (2016). Older people, sense of coherence and community. *The Handbook of Salutogenesis.*

[13] Breheny, M. & Stephens, C. (2009). I sort of pay back in my own little way: managing independence and social connectedness through reciprocity. *Ageing & Society, (29),* 1295–1313.

[14] Berry, 1992. Ibid.

prejudice against old people, history, parental authority, religious faith, sexual discipline, manual work, rural people and rural life, anything local or small or inexpensive." He concluded that "the triumph of the industrial economy" would be the fall of community.

In 2000, Harvard Professor Robert Putman[15] wrote that a "rip current" of self-absorption was tearing apart our civic engagement. As of the new millennium, Putman insists the United States has undergone an unprecedented social collapse.

In 2006, Galston and Lopez noted that instead of community, "the principal of individual choice has emerged as our central value."[16] This self-centeredness may not be limited to the United States. Globally, research shows "a rise in narcissism, and this suggests that people are becoming more isolated and focused on themselves, rather than others." Wilson and Simson remain suspicious that "as the market has become more pervasive…the range of opportunities to develop nonmarket skills and dispositions has narrowed."[17] Wennersten agrees, noting that, "For many Americans, all that is left to transact in the American community is the purchase of a more expensive automobile or house."[18]

In 2018, Johann Hari writes that most causes of depression are actually a result of loss of human connection.[19] Though he recognizes the biological causes of depression, he believes that disconnections from other people, respect, meaningful values, and the natural world have contributed more to the rise of depression around the world. I wanted to know if declining community in the U.S. motivated Baby Boomers to move to Mexico. To do this, I

---

[15] Putnam, 2000. Ibid.

[16] Simson & Wilson, 2006. Ibid.

[17] Simson & Wilson, 2006. Ibid.

[18] Wennersten, 2008. Ibid.

[19] Hari, J. (2018). Lost Connections: Why You're Depressed and How to Find Hope. London: Bloomsbury.

created a single definition of community by combining similar definitions found online.[20] My collective definition of community is: A group of people, living or working in close proximity to one another, who through their shared values feel a sense of interpersonal connectedness and belonging. I want to make it clear that my definition is about both people and place (while recognizing new types of digital and remote communities).

From the literature referenced above, we can similarly combine like definitions and measure good community through the following five variables: individual freedom, trust, dependability of the group, meaningful participation, and respect.

The survey data show that Baby Boomers who migrate to Mexico express greater perceptions of good community on all five measures than what they experience back home.

- 32% of Mexico Boomers believe Mexico provides more individual freedom to create civic activities when compared to the U.S. - 40% thought it was about the same.
- About 50% of Mexico Boomers believe there were higher levels of trust in Mexico than in the U.S. - About 30% thought it was the same.
- 53% of respondents believed they had a more dependable group in Mexico than in the U.S. - About 35% thought it was the same.
- Almost 60% of those surveyed believed that there were more opportunities for meaningful participation in their Mexico community than back in the U.S. - About 30% thought it was the same.

---

[20] Community. (2019, December 12) In *Wikipedia.*

- 88% believed that seniors received more respect in Mexico than in the U.S.

Additionally, 80% of the Mexico Boomers believed their philanthropic efforts went further in Mexico. Three out of four respondents said they had participated in a civic group or community service project over the last 12 months (compared to 25% of Baby Boomers back in the United States).[21] Maybe this is because, when compared to the United States, 75% of Mexico Boomers believed that "some good could actually be accomplished when working with others in Mexico."

Perhaps these philanthropic and volunteer efforts are explained by Mexico Boomers' sense of personal identity. Over half the survey respondents said their personal identity is strongly tied to the region where they live (only 4% said their sense of personal identity was not at all influenced by living in Mexico). When asked which aspects of the region they would be most likely to take action to preserve, the physical environment, local culture, and local community were the top three answers. Land development, pollution, and a growing population were the top three perceived regional threats.

Finally, with regard to personal threats, despite all of the Mexican drug violence depicted on the news, 44% of Mexico Boomers said they still feel safer in Mexico than the U.S., while 41% said they felt about the same. Forty-two percent said there was less crime where they lived in Mexico, with about 40% saying it was the same. Interestingly, the second most unanimous agreement in the entire survey comes from the 82% of Mexico Boomers who think

---

[21] Corporation for National and Community Service and the National Conference on Citizenship. (2017). Data show U.S. volunteer rates dipping. *Nonprofit Business Advisor, 329*, 5-8.

there is less of a threat of terrorism in Mexico than there is in the United States, even though the U.S. spends more than all other countries combined on anti-terrorism efforts.[22]

In a way, good community also promotes individualism, in that it allows individuals the ability to pursue their wants and desires, unimpeded by their physical and social surroundings. And not only does good community allow it, but it actually makes those pursuits easier (and perhaps faster) because of the support and encouragement of the other members. For example, a community of writers will make space for writing, encourage review and discussion, and (hopefully) produce better individual books. This has also been the case for artists, who have a long history of forming communes to elevate their learning and their craft.[23]

Place is also about geography and amenities. Do our physical surroundings make it easier or harder to be the people we want to be? Are we inspired by what we see outside? Is it easy to get from place to place? Do we have the supplies we need close at hand? Do we feel safe?

Jane Jacobs thought good communities could be found in places that are organic, serendipitous, and messy, with mixed land use and human diversity. Jacobs was a Canadian-American activist who fought a lot of the urban renewal movements of the 1950s through the 1970s.[24] The purpose of these movements was to replace urban decay with more expensive modern buildings and amenities, which theoretically would then kickstart and improve local communities.[25] Jacobs argued that these renewal movements actually destroyed

---

[22] Zucchi, K. (2018). What countries spend on Antiterrorism. *Investopedia*.

[23] Morfin, M. (2016, October 9). 10 fascinating artist colonies around the world. *Culture Trip*.

[24] Jane Jacobs. (2019, December 3). In *Wikipedia*.

[25] Urban renewal. (2019, December 3). In *Wikipedia*.

communities – through gentrification and a total disregard for the desires of the people who already lived there.[26] Further, Jacobs insisted, these developments created physical uniformity that was contrary to what most people preferred. Additionally, urban renewal introduced distinct districts for living and doing business. It resulted in the loss of neighborhood bodegas and our ability to simply walk next door to purchase what we need.[27] Instead, urban renewal spurred the growth of large chain stores, located further from our homes.

From my own experiences visiting expat enclaves in Mexico, I couldn't help but notice that these neighborhoods seemed to represent Jane Jacob's ideal type; that they were indeed organic, serendipitous, and messy, with mixed land use and human diversity. I wanted to know how much the prevalence of these factors mattered to the Mexico Boomers when they considered a place to live, and how present they were in their current neighborhoods. To that end, I created a series of questions asking about what was important when choosing a place to live. I provided 27 possible factors, including factors related to Jane Jacob's hypothesis. Some of these factors were: safety, good government, prosperity, healthy environment, weather, friendliness, and a good place to raise kids. I also asked participants to rank each factor by level of importance. I then asked participants to rank how well their current neighborhood ranked on each of those factors.

To get at the heart of Jacob's contention, I asked the Mexico Boomers if cultural diversity, vibrant community, and a culture of creativity were important factors to consider when picking a place to live. A majority of respondents (more than 70%) believed they were,

---

[26] Jacobs, J. (1992). The death and life of Great American cities. *Vintage Books.*

[27] Wang, H.L. (2017, March 10). New York City bodegas and the generations who love them. *NPR.*

with 'cultural diversity' ranked as most important. When asked how well Mexico ranked on each of those factors, a majority of respondents reported that Mexico was good or very good on these measures (57% or better), with a culture of creativity ranking highest. When asked if Mexico Boomers perceived a lot of mixing of business and housing in Mexico, 71% answered yes. None of the Mexico Boomers believed that Mexico enforced any distinct business and residential areas (as is done in the U.S.). And only 1 in 5 thought that a distinct separation between business and residential districts was important.

The data show that respondents believe that Mexico provides features in accordance with those they believe are important when choosing a place to live. In the context of this study, Jacob's variables of cultural diversity, vibrancy, and a culture of creativity were positively identified, and ranked favorably, within a community that reports having good community. Based on the data, Jacob's variables deserve consideration when examining or creating research related to good community. It is possible that the presence of these variables has the potential to improve people's perceptions of what constitutes good community.

Early in the book, I said the discovery of long established and vibrant expat communities came as a surprise. This is because my gut inclination, like most people's, was that the only reason people retire in Mexico is to save money. By now it's obvious that this is not entirely true. While people who are concerned about money do retire in Mexico, access to a good community is another important reason they not only migrate there but stay.

Baby Boomers have a lower standard of living than they expected. They also perceive more competition amongst each other for jobs and resources. This perceived competition might not make the best foundation for a good community. It also may lead to significant rates of depression among Baby Boomers.[28] One way to alleviate dissatisfaction is through community engagement.[29] Back in the U.S., very few Baby Boomers (as a percentage) practice much community engagement or report high levels of social connectedness. If you're someone who desires community and social engagement, Mexico might be for you. That's because more than half of those who live there are actively participating in community events, feel a strong personal connectedness to their community, and feel like a valuable member of those communities. Only about 1 in 10 Baby Boomers back in the U.S. feel the same way.

In addition to the social connectedness they feel, Mexico Boomers also feel connected to the geographic spaces in which they live. They describe their neighborhoods as diverse, vibrant, creative, and easy to get around. They love the physical environments and say they would work to protect them from land development, pollution, and a growing population. They feel safer in these places than they feel in the United States, and they report feeling respected as an elder, both within their expat community and by Mexico in general.

---

[28] Northwestern The Family Institute. (2018, March 29). Boom in ageing adults could overwhelm mental health care field.

[29] Halvorsen, C.J. & Emerman, J. The encore movement: Baby Boomers and older adults can be a powerful force to build community. *American Society on Aging.*

CHAPTER 10

Conclusions
Possibilities for Other Foreign Retirement
Destinations
Continued Trends in Out-Migration

After all we've explored, from a brief history of retirement around the world to the very specific motivations of Baby Boomers living in Mexico, the focus of this book has centered on answering three questions:

1. Do Baby Boomers move to Mexico because they are broke?
2. Do Baby Boomers move to Mexico because they experience age discrimination?
3. Do Baby Boomers move to Mexico in search of better communities?

Chapters 7, 8, and 9 have answered these questions through a review of original survey data collected over several years. What follows are my own conclusions based on that data, personal interviews, my travels in Mexico, and my review of the literature on Baby Boomer's finance, as well as sociological perspectives on age and community.

1. Money

Baby Boomers who move to Mexico, for the most part, are not broke. In fact, they run up the more financially secure side of the income scale (compared to their peers back home). They do, however, self-report that their financial situations feel more dire than they may be in actuality. Thus, we know that Americans with below-average wealth are not any more likely to retire in Mexico. Rather, people with higher incomes, and who tend to worry about money, are more likely to retire in Mexico. This concern about money may indeed come as a result of the 2008 financial crisis (as I originally proposed). As I discussed in Chapter 7, 20 years ago, most respondents expected that a good portion of their retirement income would come from a 401k. When asked where their money comes from now, 401k didn't even make the Top 5. The 2008 crash was right in the middle of that 20-year period and left those on the cusp of retirement with few, if any, years to recover what was lost.

Something else we know is that the Mexico Boomers are retiring about five years earlier than their U.S. counterparts. That may be due to some of the age discrimination issues discussed in Chapter 8. But while Mexico Boomers report feeling discriminated against (or alienated), few report having personally experienced this as part of finding meaningful employment.

Mexico is indeed a much cheaper place to live than the United States. In fact, most food, housing, and consumer costs are many times less expensive than back home. The low cost of living in Mexico allows those who are moderately well off to retire earlier than they could back home, without any significant consequence to their lifestyle.

I conclude that it is the low cost of living, rather than a lack of money or available U.S. employment that explains Mexico Boomers' early retirement. It seems fair to conclude that the typical Mexico Boomer has enough money to fund a traditional U.S.

retirement but chooses to start retirement earlier by moving to Mexico. Mexico Boomers don't move because they have less money than anyone else. They move to Mexico because they can retire earlier and live better there than they can in the United States. What motivates Mexico Boomers most is not money itself, but rather a certain lifestyle that prioritizes autonomy and leisure over the grind of an extended career.

2. Age Discrimination

There is certainly an overarching Mexico Boomer profile that has emerged from this book, and though not exclusive, a majority of Mexico Boomers would fit this description: A married person in their late 50s, highly educated, upper-income, liberal leaning, Democratic voting Caucasian who values a slower pace of life, a little adventure, and autonomy while still being a part of a community they can count on and that shows them respect.

I don't believe that Mexico Boomers move to Mexico because they feel unbearable age discrimination back home. I can appreciate that they perceive it, and I've already shown their perceptions are well founded and result in a host of personal and professional consequences. Rather, I believe that Mexico Boomers move to Mexico because they share the values of their contemporaries who are doing the same.

That does not mean that they do not experience ageist hostility and discomfort directed towards them. But it simply has not risen to the level of mass exodus. Rather, most of these Mexico Boomers feel like popular culture in the U.S. fails to represent their own values. This is not unusual. Historically, every generation has looked down on the next with some level of contempt.[1] In my

---

[1] Ruggeri, A. (2017, October 3). People have always whined about young adults. Here's proof. *BBC*.

interviews, Mexico Boomers described U.S. culture as "crumbling" and obsessed with shopping and looking young. A culture that focuses on consumerism and spending will not be a good fit for Baby Boomers who worry about money. And a culture that is focused on youth may not resonate with Baby Boomers who are no longer able to disguise their years with new creams and clothing. With messages that glamorize spending and youth pervasive across mass media, it's no surprise that a large number of Mexico Boomers feel alienated from American culture.[2] But is that enough to make them move away? No, I don't think so. Other than their age, Mexico Boomers still enjoy respect with regard to their race, education level, income level, and religious freedom. And while some intergenerational hostility is taking place ("Ok, Boomer"), it has not risen to a level of persecution.[3]

Conversely, I think Mexico Boomers are genuinely interested in participating in Mexican culture. While small pockets are isolated, most report values similar to their new Mexican neighbors. Almost every Mexico Boomer I met attempted to speak Spanish when talking to a local. Many had developed romantic relationships with Mexicans, and some had even formed cross-cultural business partnerships. As I wrote early on, these were not penny pinching, isolated seniors. These are vibrant people who have tried to respectfully integrate themselves into their Mexican communities and live outward, civically engaged lives. That is not to say that this does not cause some periodic strife between the two cultures, but it has not risen to the level of feeling unwelcome.

I suspect there is another reason Mexico Boomers choose Mexico over the United States. Retirement abroad creates a

---

[2] Frey, W.H. (2012, June 8). Baby Boomers had better embrace change. *The Washington Post*.

[3] Scott, H. (2019, November 13). The problem with 'OK, boomer.' *The Washington Post*.

wonderful intellectual challenge. There is so much to learn: the language, the customs, the laws, the art, even the holidays (Dia de Muertos for example). For highly educated people who crave intellectual stimulation, moving to Mexico creates an instant mental challenge (which we know from Chapter 9 can help stave off late-life cognitive decline).

A lot of the people I interviewed talked about overcoming significant personal struggles as part of their journey to Mexico. Mexico Boomers have a palatable grit – a fortitude you can feel. For those who have little patience for learning and low tolerance for embarrassment, then a Mexican retirement may not be for you. It is by no means hard, but life in Mexico doesn't just fall in around you. You have to make it happen. You have to learn to communicate. You have to make your own phone calls and look at a map. You have to ask for things you don't have the words for. You have to find your own doctor. There is no cruise concierge. And if you don't want milk in your coffee, you better learn sin leche.

3. Good Community

Imagine the last time you felt part of a good community. Perhaps it is right now, or it was as a child, safe in your parents' home. It might have been a period of your life raising your kids with neighbors or as a student in graduate school. Whenever it was, if I were to ask you to describe the physical things that made you feel welcome, it may be hard. That is the thing with good community, it's not always easy to describe, and sometimes even tougher to quantify. It's not a series of things we can check off a list, but rather a feeling, like the wind, that can be felt but hard to see, yet reassures us that we are in the middle of it, right where we need to be.

When I asked the Mexico Boomers to describe good community, they pointed to choice, individual freedom, trust, respect, meaningful participation, dependability of the group, cultural diversity, vibrancy, and a culture of creativity as things that were most important to them. Almost every Mexico Boomer agreed that if money was not an issue, they would still live in Mexico over the United States. This is because they have found a community that shares their values and where they feel respected. Yes, it was money that led them to consider retirement in Mexico, but it's good community that keeps them from returning home.

Through my interviews I've come to believe that, like Wendall Berry, Mexico Boomers believe consumerism is also ruining good community in America. A majority believe that the United States is no longer a place where strong and meaningful communities can be formed. They believe that most people in the States see others as a means to an end and that you "can't be too careful when dealing with other people in America."

In Mexico, outside the constant bombardment of U.S. media, they report a sense of peace. I cannot say whether Mexico is truly more peaceful, but I can say I understand where they are coming from. In my own travels abroad, I've experienced a similar peace whenever I enter a land with foreign language and customs. Though there may be advertising and petty arguments on the television, I am blind to them. I simply do not understand, and in a way that makes them invisible. It is this invisibility that brings me peace, not necessarily the place itself. I agree that the U.S. media is full of negativity and strife. Taking a break from it recharges my batteries, and at times leaves me thinking a foreign place may actually be better.

The Mexico Boomers value both community and individual freedom, including freedom from a barrage of American advertising. They seek out meaningful participation on projects of impact. Unlike their Sun City living contemporaries, who spend their days in closed communities playing bocce ball or attending sewing class, the Mexico Boomers focus their efforts on helping orphans, cleaning up pollution, and building libraries.[4] They are explorers who are up for new challenges. They are not looking for an easy life. They are looking for a meaningful life. They do not seek to have their time occupied by corporate retirement planners. They wish to fill their days with what matters most to them, as individuals, and to live in a place where they are recognized by their community as a person, not as a marketing demographic or source of revenue.

This research is one of the few academic studies that explores the reasons U.S. Baby Boomers migrate to Mexico, but it has its limits. First, it only accounts for those Baby Boomers who have moved to Mexico, who have an internet connection, who maintain a social media presence, who are open to be being surveyed or interviewed, and who are happy to have their opinions known. It doesn't take into account the perceptions of the countless Baby Boomers who move to Mexico to truly get away from anything American, which itself is an unexplored motivation and not part of this book. The people I surveyed and interviewed were not trying to disappear. They were not trying to break themselves entirely free from their ties to the U.S. or their national heritage. In addition to their new Mexican neighbors and friends, they continue to seek out other Americans and maintain ties to U.S. news, politics, holidays, and traditions. At the end of the day, they have not become Mexicans. They are Americans living in Mexico who are happier in Mexico than they were back home.

The second limitation of this book is that it does not explore Mexican perceptions of Americans moving into their neighborhoods. That is not to say that the topic doesn't matter. In fact, it is very important as to whether this trend can survive. There are many

---

[4] Lake Chapala Society. Volunteers are at the heart of LCS.

factors that might give these Mexican hosts pause, including supply and demand of housing, strains on natural resources, and overcrowding. There are also threats to the existing Mexican culture and identity via the import of businesses aimed at serving the expectations of U.S. customers, including Costco, Home Depot, and Walmart.[5] Like Jane Jacobs insisted, good communities are messy and vibrant. The arrival of these big box and home improvement stores can do a lot to standardize and simplify what started as an eclectic mix of architecture, food, and commerce. The irony is that this eclectic mix that was so attractive to expats is now threatened by their very arrival – and the companies that have followed them south.

To date, U.S. expat communities in Mexico have been successfully sustained for nearly 75 years. But in the last decade, the number of U.S. expats living in Mexico jumped from 1 million to 1.5 million. Though exact numbers are hard to calculate, this research (and my own experience) leads me to believe a significant portion of this increase is U.S. Baby Boomers migrating to Mexico.

Nearly 20 years ago, Dr. Truly revealed that positively motivated U.S. seniors moved to Lake Chapala in search of tolerant, egalitarian, casual, and unstructured communities.[6] And though he writes that "traditional factors," such as climate and cost of living, initially attracted them to Mexico, "eventually, their appreciation for the Mexican lifestyle and the unique nature of the foreign community had kept them in the area." Baby Boomers arriving across the country today seem to be no different. During most of my personal interviews, money or the cost of living was never the first thing people wanted to talk about. Instead, they wanted me to know how

---

[5] Croucher, S.L. (2009). *The other side of the fence: American migrants in Mexico.* Austin: University of Texas Press.

[6] Truly, 2002. Ibid.

much happier they were now than they had ever been before. They wanted to tell me about the friends they made and how kind Mexicans had been to them. They talked about experiencing a sense of belonging and peace that had been hard to find in the United States. And they were not secretive or greedy about what they discovered. More often, they acted as advocates for their new way of life, expressing frustration that their friends and family back home wouldn't believe that what they were saying was true. It will be interesting to see if this 20-year trend of embracing community over finance endures as more Baby Boomers at the tail-end of the generation start to retire, facing even deeper financial hardship than those who came before.

Just 12 years ago, Wennersten uncovered six motivations that help explain expatriate out-migration across all generations: (1) Transnational and Lifestyle Realization, (2) Cultural Dissonance, (3) Entrepreneurial Advancement, (4) Settlement and Re-adaptation, (5) Economic Dissent, and (6) Expanding Gender Domains.[7] With the exception of Entrepreneurial Advancement and Settlement and Re-adaptation, these motivations also hold true for today's Mexico Boomers. Without question, these individuals are seeking out destinations that provide a low cost of living. But they do so because they are uncertain about what it means to be an American. They seek something different than the restrictions they feel in their home society. And women who move to Mexico are transformed by the freedom they feel from traditional gender roles and the relief that comes from being in a place where they can financially afford to go it alone.

Baby Boomers in Mexico have been successful because of good economics, good communities, and their willingness to integrate into existing Mexican culture. Community planners in other

---

[7] See Chapter 5 to revisit Wennersten's motivational definitions.

foreign retirement destinations should carefully consider this combination of economics and good community. Additionally, they must understand how open their existing native communities are to receiving an influx of older Americans. Without local buy-in and cooperation, there can be little hope of becoming the next successful international retirement destination. Foreign governments and developers must have (or be willing to create) physical spaces that encourage choice, individual freedom, trust, respect, meaningful participation, dependability of the group, cultural diversity, vibrancy, and a culture of creativity. This research shows this is the best way to attract and keep Baby Boomer retirees and their American dollars. And those dollars could be well worth it. Investopia estimates retired couples spend about $2200 per month (or $26,400/year) on expenses while living abroad. If Belize or Panama could find a way to attract 5000 retired couples to a community, that could inject $132 million dollars a year into that local economy. This figure is not so farfetched. Consider the Mexican city of San Miguel de Allende for example. Just five years ago the U.S. expat population was estimated to be 5,000. Today, that figure has swollen to 12,500. While economics certainly played a role in this growth, the existence of a strong community is what's making them stay.

Back in the United States, policymakers should take note of just how attractive international retirement has become. Although the financial collapse of 2008 was over 10 years ago, Baby Boomers continue to face tough economic times. But now they have options. It's not just Mexico. Expat retirement communities are springing up all over the globe, including Panama, Portugal, and Columbia.[8] The ramifications of a growing exodus of retirees could include a reduction in volunteerism and mentoring back in the U.S. (a pool

---

[8] Nova, A. (2019, November 28). Here's where you can retire nicely on just $30,000 a year… outside the U.S. *CNBC News*.

traditionally made up of well-educated retired persons). For those who remain, poorly planned, age-dense neighborhoods that do not provide good community could result in poor physical and mental health among retirees and put further strain on the U.S. healthcare system. And because Baby Boomers still control the largest portion of wealth inside the United States, the transfer of those dollars into foreign economies could have severe consequences for the economy back home.[9] What this book suggests is that once Baby Boomers decide to leave the U.S and find communities that balance their economic and social needs, it's almost impossible to get them back.

---

[9] Marketing Charts. (2019, April 8). Baby Boomers possess the majority of U.S. household wealth.

APPENDIX

Where They Live
>   Tijuana - The Old Wild Side
>   San Miguel de Allende - The Heart of Mexico
>   Mexicali - The Silicon Border
>   Ensenada - A Pearl in the Pacific
>   Lake Chapala - An Artist's Retreat
>   Puerto Vallarta - The Salty Foot
>   Merida - The Capital of Culture
>   Tulum - The Mayan Mecca

Top Five Expat Communities

In 2019, between 1 and 1.5 million U.S. expats call Mexico home.[1] Mexico has the largest population of U.S. expats found anywhere in the world. Although expats can be found living in communities across Mexico, five cities top the list: Tijuana, San Miguel de Allende, Mexicali, Ensenada, and Chapala.[2] In addition to profiling these five cities, I've added a few more expat hotspots that are growing fast: Puerto Vallarta, Merida, and Tulum.

---

[1] International Living. Ibid.
[2] Courtney. (2019) Where do Mexico's 1 million U.S. expats live? *Viva Tropical.*

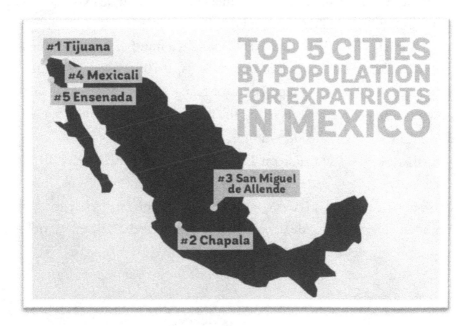

TOP 5 CITIES BY POPULATION FOR EXPATRIOTS IN MEXICO

#1 Tijuana
#4 Mexicali
#5 Ensenada
#3 San Miguel de Allende
#2 Chapala

Tijuana: No Longer the Wild City to the South

With a population of 1.3 million residents, Tijuana is becoming a business, political, and cultural focal point in Mexico. Tijuana is located on the Baja California Gold Coast, directly at the Mexican border with the U.S. Because Tijuana – TJ – is uniquely situated as part of the international San Diego-Tijuana metroplex, the city is home to an eclectic mix of expats. The Tijuana border point is the busiest in the world. There are approximately 300,000 crossings daily.

Baby Boomers and younger, working Americans are migrating to TJ in ever-increasing numbers. As of 2015, Tijuana is home to the largest number of U.S. expats found anywhere in Mexico. While some younger Americans are drawn to the hip cultural scene in TJ, many more relocate their residences for financial reasons. These younger expats tend to live in TJ and work in San Diego, vastly improving their standard of living. Growing numbers of younger, working Americans and Baby Boomers creates a unique expat community that is vibrant and robust.

Many Baby Boomers likely maintain a number of perceptions about TJ that are holdovers from the 1960s, 1970s, 1980s. On the one hand, Tijuana had a reputation for being a "seedy place" – a wild town where people slipped across the border from the United States for a walk on the wild side.[3] In time, that perception was overshadowed by reporting on Tijuana as a violent, lawless city. In fact, between 1990 and the early 2000s, the Tijuana Cartel, a narco trafficking organization, was considered one of the most violent criminal enterprises in Mexico. The eradication of the Tijuana Cartel represented one of Mexico's prime victories in its war on narco trafficking. Since 2006, TJ has been free from the scourge of the Tijuana Cartel and its associated crime and violence. The U.S. State Department reports that there is no evidence to suggest U.S. citizens or expats are targets of crime in TJ.

In the aftermath of the 9/11 terrorist attacks, security was tightened at the U.S.-Mexico border in Tijuana. Initially after this incident, a number of expats who resided in TJ and throughout Baja California, headed back to the States. However, the Great Recession of 2008reversed this trend, and expats migrated back to TJ. In recent years, TJ experienced something of a rebirth – a sort of Baja California renaissance – that resulted in less seediness, less crime and more culture, class, and vibrancy.

Crime rates in TJ have dropped dramatically in recent years. The Citizen Council for Public Safety and Criminal historically, consistently rated TJ one of the 50 deadliest cities in the world. In recent years, TJ has been off the list. As crime rates dropped, the

---

[3] Tijuana. Retrieved from: https://allaboutbaja.com/baja-cities/tijuana/

number of cultural, recreational, dining, shopping, and other opportunities expanded.

While younger expats tend to reside in locations throughout TJ, Baby Boomers are found in comfortable enclaves. These enclaves have developed along the outskirts of the city itself, with some upscale ones dotting the beaches of the Gold Coast.

Like younger expats, Baby Boomer retirees also enjoy TJ's close proximity to the U.S. Its border location permits Boomer expats greater ease in staying physically connected to their families in the United States. In addition, it is far easier for them to tend to business in the States as necessary.

Additionally, Boomers are attracted to the city because of its climate. TJ is described as having a Mediterranean climate, more temperate than some inland communities because of its location on the Pacific coastline, resulting in a consistently pleasant environment.

San Miguel de Allende: The Heart of Mexico

A full 10% of the population of San Miguel de Allende is expats, the majority of whom hail originally from the United States and Canada. As of 2019, 12,000 U.S. and Canadian expats call San Miguel home.[4] With an increasing number of U.S. expats in San Miguel, locals joke that the city has become more like Disneyland than Mexico.

San Miguel is located in central Mexico, a 10-hour drive from the U.S. border, in the state of Guanajuato. Tourists frequent the well-preserved city center and its elegant buildings that date back to the 16th and 17th century. The grandeur of the city provides a stunning backdrop for Boomer expats who enjoy the cultural, entertainment, and recreational activities around the district.

---

[4] Lange, D. (2014, June 30). Aging out of place in San Miguel, Mexico. *Senior Planet.*

A noticeable number of first-wave expats into San Miguel, particularly from the U.S., were artists.[5] Even today as a wider range of expats move into the city, parts of San Miguel maintain the feel of an artists' colony.

In addition to its favorable cost of living and cultural offerings, San Miguel scores big with expats because of its mild climate and low crime rate. It also has an international airport within a 90-minute drive, making it relatively easy to reach from the United States. This is a key consideration for a good number of retirees who have children and grandchildren in the States.

San Miguel epitomizes one of the three trends that encourage American retirees to emigrate to Mexico. In San Miguel, American expats have a tremendous influence on the city's overall scene. From organic bistros to clothing stores that feature American fare and entertainment with a U.S. flare, strolling through many parts of San Miguel it can be hard to tell if you actually departed the States. Although this is appealing to some expats, a number of Mexican nationals residing in San Miguel derisively refer to this trend as "Disneyfication" of their community.[6]

Two other trends are less obvious in San Miguel, but they are evident in other communities popular with U.S. expats discussed in this book. There are sections of San Miguel where U.S. expats can blend into the local population or scene, thoroughly intermingling with Mexican nationals. In addition, there are some enclaves within the city that are populated by U.S. retirees who migrated to the city and choose to live in cohesive clusters with others from the States.

---

[5] Willens, M. (2017, July 12). The second life of San Miguel de Allende. *The Daily Beast.*

[6] Lonely Planet. San Miguel de Allende is cobbled streets and culture.

Mexicali: Boomers at the Silicon Border

Located on the Mexican border with the United States, Mexicali is the capital of the state of Baja California.[7] The city of Mexicali itself has a population of about 700,000, and the metro area is home to approximately 1 million residents.

Mexicali has an arid, desert climate. Although Mexicali is located relatively close to Tijuana, average temperatures in Mexicali tend to be warmer throughout the year than in Tijuana because TJ is located on the Pacific Ocean.

The 21st century has transformed Mexicali from a largely agrarian community into the Mexican counterpart to the Silicon Border. With the growth of high-tech enterprises in Mexicali, including a burgeoning aerospace industry, the cultural opportunities, dining options, retail outlets and recreational activities in and around the city are akin to what is found in booming corridors within the United States.

Mexicali is also considered the most ethnically diverse city in Mexico. It includes a broad mix of expatriates from around the globe, including North America, Europe, the Middle East, and China.[8] The city has a large population of Chinese expats, some that hail directly from China itself and others that have ended up in Mexicali after initially living in the United States. Chinese influence is significant in Mexicali. The city is home to a large Chinatown district and Cantonese cuisine is the most common dining fare after native Mexican dishes. In other words, as of this time in Mexicali it is the Chinese who are leaving an imprint on the city rather than expats from the U.S. or other nations.

A border town like Tijuana, Mexicali is located conveniently for U.S. expats who must tend to business or visit family in the States

---

[7] Mexicali. Retrieved from: https://allaboutbaja.com/baja-cities/mexicali/
[8] Mexicali. Ibid.

with relative ease. The U.S. State Department reports that violent crime along the U.S. border, including in the Mexicali area, nearly always occurs between individuals involved in narco trafficking. U.S. expats residing in Mexicali are deemed unlikely criminal targets. This particularly is true within the city limits of Mexicali itself, where the vast majority of U.S. Boomer expats reside.

Ensenada: A Pearl at the Pacific

Located in Baja California, about 80 miles south of San Diego, locals consider Ensenada to be the "Cinderella of the Pacific."[9] The city is located along the Pacific shoreline and is a cruise ship destination along Mexico's Gold Coast.

Ensenada has a population of about 450,000 residents. The city is described as a beach community featuring mid-rise residential and commercial structures. Multi-unit residential properties tend to be the norm for expats in Ensenada.

Ensenada is a prime destination for three types of American expats: retirees who migrate and make Ensenada their primary residence, snowbirds who winter in the city in a manner akin to South Florida and Phoenix-Scottsdale in the States, and younger American expats who come to the city to escape higher costs of living in the U.S. These younger Americans live in Ensenada but work in California. An estimated 20,000 U.S. expats reside in Ensenada, the majority of whom are retirees.

In addition to being able to make their retirement dollars go further, Boomers settle in Ensenada because of its climate. Nestled along the Pacific coastline, residents of Ensenada enjoy consistently warm temperatures throughout the year. Essentially a beach-front

---

[9] Ensenada, Mexico.Trip Advisor, retrieved from: https://www.tripadvisor.com/Tourism-g150770-Ensenada_Ensenada_Municipality_Baja_California-Vacations.html

community, the city is relatively humid throughout much of the year, and sea breezes temper the climate.

U.S. expats in Ensenada are not targeted for criminal activity and are not exposed to a higher level risk of crime because of their nationality, according to the U.S. State Department. Boomers living in Ensenada are advised to exercise the same precautions they would follow if living in the United States.

Chapala: An Artist's Retreat

Lake Chapala is Mexico's largest body of freshwater. The lake is located just 30 miles south of the city of Guadalajara, in the state of Jalisco. After Mexico City, Guadalajara is Mexico's second largest city, with a metro population of about 5.5 million. Lake Chapala came to international attention in the late 19th century. President Diaz conceptualized Lake Chapala as Mexico's international tourist destination.[10] The arrival of the rail lines quickly attracted North American and European visitors. But in 1910, the Mexican Revolution burst Lake Chapala's first tourism bubble.[11]

The area would not see a significant return of tourists until the 1940s. During Lake Chapala's revival, the area became a haven for writers, painters, poets, and photographers. It received some of the world's most renowned authors, including Ernest Hemmingway, D.H. Lawrence, and George Bernard Shaw. In addition to its international tourism, Lake Chapala remained the weekend getaway spot for the middle and upper-class residents of Guadalajara.

The Lake Chapala region currently consists of three main villages, including Jocotepec on the northwest corner of the lake and Ajijic and Chapala further east. The year-round permanent

---

[10] Truly, 2002. Ibid.

[11] Burton, T. (2008). *Lake Chapala Through the Ages: An anthology of travelers' tales*. Sombrero Books: Ladysmith BC. Canada.

population is approximately 40,000 residents, which 5,000 to 6,000 are English-speaking expatriates. Seasonal winter influxes elevate this number to approximately 12,000. In 1996, the American Consulate reported this number could be as high as 40,000, though local residents believe this number is a bit exaggerated[12].

The Lake Chapala Society was formed on January 15, 1955, with 31 members and a mission of helping out expatriates new to the area. Two of the most prominent founding members were Brig. General John Paul Ratay and a woman named Neill James. Ratay believed a society was needed to assist both the locals and the influx of military personnel arriving on the GI bill. During my visit to the Lake Chapala Society, I was told that GI's enrolled in local universities because they were far cheaper than U.S. universities and the excess money could be used to achieve a comfortable living that was not available in the United States.

Neill James was a contemporary of Amelia Earhart and is considered a pioneering woman of travel and journalism. James was born in Grenada, Mississippi in 1885, and no one could ever keep her quiet.[13] She loved to travel. At one point, she lived with and documented the lives of the Ainu people of northern Japan. In 1941, she was climbing the Volcano Paricutin when it erupted, badly injuring her. She was taken to the village Ajijic on the Lake Chapala shore to rest and recover. During a year-long recovery, she fell in love with the people and the geography of the region. She established Ajijic as her permanent address and transformed the area into "an art center of international focus." Neill founded the first library in Chapala. She taught cooking, developed water purification systems, and installed electricity and telephone lines. Neill was always

---

12 Truly, 2002. Ibid.

13 Lake Chapala Society. (2009). Membership Directory 2009.

considered kind and caring. In fact, she used a large inheritance from her father to send the most talented local children on through the university system.

During the 1970s, industrial pollution threatened Lake Chapala's tourism. Lake Chapala Society members banded together to clean the lake up, as it serves as the main water source for both Mexico City and Guadalajara. The main influx of water to the lake comes from the Rio Lerma River. Large industrial and agricultural complexes upstream dumped pollutants and toxins into the Rio Lerma, including mercury, fertilizers, and lead. These toxins eventually settled in the water and shores of Lake Chapala. By 2002, Mexico's National Water Commission (CNA) reported that only 8% of the water in Lake Chapala was considered "acceptable" for drinking. The remaining 92% was either moderately or highly polluted.[14]

Today the Lake Chapala Society has over known 3700 members. According to the Lake Chapala Society's website, the society has three missions. The first is to help the local community with an emphasis on children and education. Second, the society assists expatriates as they transition to Mexican living. Third, the society provides social, health, and educational services for expatriates.[15] According to their membership directory, the Lake Chapala Society offers or sponsors over 40 monthly programs. Some of them include the Lakeside Theater, which has been bringing English language performances to the area for over 45 years. There is also a Music Appreciation Society, which has been bringing international entertainment to the area for over 21 years. Other groups include the Culinary Art Society of Ajijic, the Masons, the

---

[14] Amigos del Lago (2009). Data Presented at the *2002 Living Lakes Conference in South Africa*, Retrieved http://www.amigosdelago.org/lago/pollution_2002-e.htm

[15] Lake Chapala Society Website: www.lakechapalasociety.org

Shriners, an Organic Farm Club, Spanish language group, a writing group, and yoga. A Saturday schedule includes a children's art program, an art fundraiser, Qi Gong, and a pottery class.

Puerto Vallarta: Hogar del pie salado (home of the salty foot)

Known as a resort location, Puerto Vallarta (also known as PV to English speakers or simply Vallarta) is located on the western side of Mexico on the Pacific coast of Jalisco. This city has a population of just over 250,000, and it caters to tourists, so there is a lot to see and do.

Vallarta wasn't always a hopping destination. In the 1960s, it was mostly a sleepy little town that few Americans had given much thought to, but all that changed when actor Richard Burton filmed The Night of the Iguana in the area.[16] His then-rumored, now-confirmed affair with Elizabeth Taylor received extensive media coverage that put Vallarta on the radar. Now, visitors can even stay in the home the couple bought together, which now functions as a hotel with a restaurant named Iguana in honor of the film.

Beginning in the 1970s, the city consciously worked on building its image as a resort destination, and following President Richard Nixon's treaty negotiations with Mexican President Gustavo Diaz Ordaz in the city, many hotels began popping up to take advantage of ongoing interest in the region.[17] Since then, the city has continued to thrive and grow as a popular destination.

It's no wonder that Vallarta has continued to attract so many visitors. With near-perfect temperatures (it shares its latitude with

---

[16] Marcus, L. (2016, January 11). A former Elizabeth Taylor/Richard Burton Home is now the coolest new hotel in Puerto Vallarta. *Conde Nast Traveler.*

[17] Nixon Foundation. (2014, August 20). President Nixon's state visit to Mexico – 8.20.1970.

Hawaii and has comparable weather) ranging from 70-85 degrees and gorgeous beaches and jungles, the city is something of a paradise.

The city has a reputation for being one of the safest in Mexico, which is another reason people are so comfortable getting out and about here.[18] Those who are looking to stay in the thick of things will find plenty of activities and bustling restaurants in the heart of the city's tourism corridor, but there are also secluded hotels (some that can only be reached by boat) that promise a relaxing and quiet experience.

Because the city is built heavily around visitors, the official tourism site[19] is extensive and features attractions specifically geared for couples, families, business trips, and LGBT visitors.

If you're looking for hospitality and well-thought-out amenities, PV has you covered. Because of how attractive as the city is for tourists, some just can't find it in them to go back home. Puerto Vallarta is home to a large number of expats, and they are happy to sing the praises of their new locale. The city is highly accessible by both air and sea, making it a popular destination for those looking to move to Mexico but would still like to stay connected.[20] While many of the expats who call the PV home are members of the elite celebrity class, there has also been an uptick in average retirees. The cost of living here is higher than other Mexican expat locales, but it is still affordable compared to many American cities.

The city has a great reputation for expats and has been named both the "Friendliest City in the World" and the "Best Place to Retire."[21] There are private health clinics offering US-quality

---

[18] Brodsky, K. (2018, February 14). Puerto Vallarta: Get this Mexican beach to yourself. *CNN.*

[19] https://visitpuertovallarta.com

[20] Mexperience. Ibid.

[21] Squire, B. (2017, September 13). Living the dream – The Puerto Vallarta lifestyle. *Banderas News.*

healthcare, and the plethora of expats and native Mexicans flocking to the city ensure lots of easily accessible opportunities for daily shopping. Those who have chosen to call the city home gush about the art, the food, and the friendliness.

Merida: The Capital of Culture

While many Mexican tourist attractions and homes to American expats are located on the coast, Merida, is an inland city with a lot to appreciate. In fact, this amazing city has been named the American Capital of Culture – twice.[22] It was first awarded the honor in 2000 and was just crowned the winner again in 2017; it is the only city to have a dual win to its name.

Located in the northwestern part of Yucatan (and serving as its capital city), Merida's history is rooted in Mayan culture and is shaped by colonial influences. The Mayan influence is everywhere, from architecture to cuisine to the laidback camaraderie of the people themselves.[23] Merida is also home to the Gran Museo del Mundo Maya, a breathtaking art and history museum.

The colonial influence of the region is also strong, with many of the haciendas that were once inhabited by Spanish conquerors being repurposed into tourist attractions.[24] These gorgeous plantation houses have been converted into hotels and spas, maintaining a piece of this tense history with a modern-day twist.

The city is large, home to almost 900,000 residents. Its weather remains pretty consistently warm with an average between 63 and 97 year-round, with the warmest peak in May and June. One amazing natural attraction of Merida is the "cenotes" (meaning

---

[22] Yucatan Expat life. (2016, January 9). Merida wins Cultural Capital title – again.

[23] Capmeil, J. & Wilentz, A. (2012, June 26). Merida in Bloom: The food, art, design, and Mayan culture of Merida. *Conde Nast Traveler.*

[24] Henderson, J. (2017, July 25). How the crumbling haciendas of the Yucatan have been reinvented as ultra-stylish hideaways. *The Telegraph.*

sinkholes). These natural geological features create amazing caves and pools to explore. Some of them boast turquoise water and glimpses of a rare eyeless fish. Others have underwater caverns and waterfalls. These unforgettable sights will be sure to make for a meaningful vacation stop.

Because it doesn't lie along the coast, Merida has only a moderate expat penetration.[25] The population that does call this city home has a lot to say in its favor, though.

For one thing, the cost of living is lower than many other areas. It appeals to urbanites, as the population is dense, and the hustle and bustle are constant. It is a melting pot of cultures, reflected in both its history and its present. If you're looking to stay busy, this city will offer you a continuous parade of festivals, concerts, and art displays. You'll always have something to do!

The switch from an American lifestyle to one in Merida is often not as difficult because of the city's large size and colonial history. There are many modern amenities built into the scene. Land and housing both remain very affordable, and excellent healthcare is available. In fact, there are world-class private hospitals that rival hospitals anywhere in the world.

One of the most praised parts of Merida is its local markets.[26] Booths filled with fresh, exotic fruits and vegetables line the streets. And cooking classes abound to help you get acquainted with the cuisine.

Upon first glance, this city may not seem as appealing for expats as the paradise-like locales that draw other retirees and wanderlust travelers, but Merida has a charm all its own and a vibrant history and culture that can't be matched anywhere else.

---

[25] Mexperience. Ibid.

[26] Walsh, N. (2017, November 16). A guide to Merida, Mexico: 10 reasons to visit now. *Forbes*.

Tulum: A Mayan Mecca

Tulum is located on the eastern edge of the Yucatan Peninsula and boasts a vibrant culture with rich historical significance as well as amazing weather that makes it an excellent place for expats and tourists alike.

Tulum's name is a nod to its place in history.[27] Tulum means "wall," and it reflects the Mayan and Zama civilizations that built great structures into the limestone cliffs overlooking the shores of this coastal city. Some of these structures (like the Castillo and the Temple of the Frescoes) are still present today. The ruins are a tourist attraction.

Tulum is a small but growing community with a population around 20,000. Its proximity to destination hot spot Cancun (about 90 minutes away) has given it a reputation that exceeds its small size. It is known for its "zen" feel, with gorgeous beaches, vegan restaurants, and plenty of places to practice yoga.[28] This is a place where someone can get in touch with their inner selves, a meaningful community, and the beauty of nature all at once.

Straddling touristy and authentic, there are lots of places to eat and things to do in Tulum, so it has enough to keep residents busy without the hustle and bustle of full-blown tourist destinations. There is an eco-centric hotel zone, and plenty of beachside eateries.[29]

One thing that makes Tulum attractive is its weather. In addition to the beautiful beaches and lush jungles, the weather tends to stay between 60 and 85 degrees most months of the year. The average for the warmest months (July and August) is about 90 degrees, making this paradise warm without sweltering.

---

[27] Cartwright, M. (2015, February 3). Tulum. *Ancient History Encyclopedia.*

[28] Siegel, E. (2017, February 8). The 6 things you need to do in Tulum, Mexico. *Forbes.*

[29] Odell, K. (2019, October 30). The 18 essential Tulum restaurants. *Eater.*

This weather draws many expats to Tulum, including Canadian expat Michelle Bradshaw who cites an escape from the harsh Canadian winters and the laid-back atmosphere as her primary draws to the city.[30] She also notes that her cost of living has decreased dramatically, crediting the fresh markets and her avoidance of malls that drop her overall expenses by nearly 70%.

Bradshaw also says that the locals are friendly and welcoming to expats, helping them adapt to the culture and learn the language so they can take advantage of the many activities Tulum has to offer, including scuba diving and ruin climbing.

Expat Dianne Harper shares similar views.[31] She found the white sand beaches and beautiful palm trees to be the perfect fit for her family's retirement. Now that she has a house tucked away in the jungle, she is happy to say that she also has access to a banana grove, something she didn't even know she wanted in her life.

Tulum is a fast-growing expat location, and that means that it has a lot to offer in the way of amenities. Many expats are digital nomads who work abroad virtually, giving them freedom to enjoy all Tulum has to offer.

Amazon delivery makes shopping easy, and plenty of local shopping outlets are available for groceries and day-to-day necessities. Healthcare, too, is very affordable; doctor's visits are much less expensive than U.S. healthcare.

Overall, this gorgeous and historical city has a lot to offer inhabitants both in the way of scenery and community. It's a great time to get involved in this growing spot.

---

[30] Bradshaw, M. (2015, November 5). Interview: Canadian expat Michelle on living in Tulum, Mexico. *Live and Invest Overseas Conferences.*

[31] Harper, D. (2016, August 15). Why this expat chose Tulum, Mexico, for retirement. *Live and Invest Overseas Conferences.*

ACKNOWLEDGEMENTS

There have been countless people who have supported this research and this book. I'd like to thank Sommer Luther, Samuel Gordon, Matt Huggins, Spencer Reedy, Elizabeth Stoycheff, Mike Broemmel, my EO family, Jimbo and Iven, Jay and Heidi, Leon Duran, and everyone else who offered words of encouragement and a little bit of proof reading. Adios Amigos. Los amo a todos. Ya sabes.

ABOUT THE AUTHOR

Travis Scott Luther is a Denver, Colorado writer, speaker, and entrepreneur. He received his Masters in Sociology from the University of Colorado Denver. He is a former Adjunct Professor of Entrepreneurship at MSU Denver and currently serves as Director for MSU Denver's RoadFounders College Business Incubator. He is a member of Entrepreneurs Organization (EO) where he served as National Chair for the 2019 Global Student Entrepreneurship Awards.

Luther first became interested in Baby Boomers retiring in Mexico during graduate school. His Masters Thesis research contributed to the content in this book. He continues to be interested in U.S. expatriates retiring all over the world and continues to monitor those who have chosen Mexico.

www.TravisLuther.com

www.MightyBuffalo.com

WITHDRAWN
HOWARD COUNTY LIBRARY

9 781647 640026